Milady
1295 ✓
2/88

New Image For Men

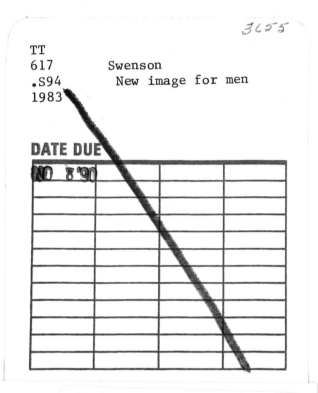

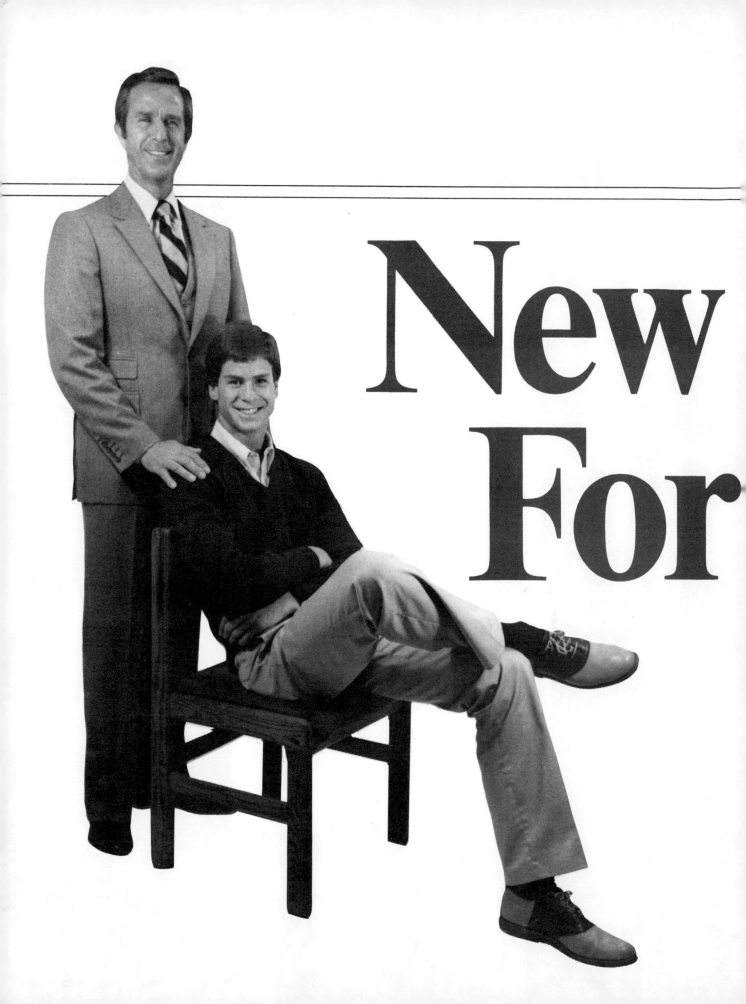

New For

Marge Swenson and Gerrie Pinckney

Image Men

Color & Wardrobe

Illustrations by
Gabe Gomez

FASHION
ACADEMY INC.

2850 Mesa Verde Drive East
Costa Mesa, California 92626
Telephone (714) 979-8073

Copyright © 1983 Marge Swenson, Gerrie Pinckney
ISBN: 0-9610190-0-X

Printed in U.S.A.
by Queen Beach Printers, Inc.
Long Beach, California

With appreciation for their loyalty and encouragement, we dedicate this book to our many clients, the Fashion Academy Certified Consultants, our friends and families.

ACKNOWLEDGEMENTS

Many thanks to Gabe Gomez for direction, art and graphics; to Joel Swenson for long hours behind the camera; to Perry Zachary and Samuel J. Wiggins, hair stylists; to Larry Smith from Lido Optical for use of eye-glasses; and Greg Chapman, clothier par excellence, for advice and encouragement, and Jim Smith, cartoonist.

Because of the tremendous and wide-spread response to our first book, "Your New Image", many independent and professional organizations have adopted that text as instructional material. We have received a flood of inquiries and pre-orders for "New Image For Men; Color & Wardrobe". Although we are very pleased by this enthusiastic response, the authors and the Fashion Academy Inc. cannot endorse any particular program of instruction with the exception of Fashion Academy certified consultants. This is not to imply that we do not recognize the quality of many other programs and hope that both books will continue to be of value to all who use them.

Before engaging professional assistance, we would urge the reader to consider the background and credibility of the consult-ant, just as one would in any other field.

Contents

THE MEN IN OUR PHOTOS

We are grateful to our clients, friends and family
who patiently sat for portraits and pictures.

Buddy R. Bearbower
Jim Brehany
Tim Brown
James Buchmiller
Ralph H. Castleton
Kevin Childress
Robert Corsaut
Troy Cox
Dr. C. D. "Mickey" Downs
Reed Farnsworth
Gabe Gomez
Ken W. Hall
Ned T. Hall
Phil Hanf
Webb Harwell

Ken Iverson
Mark Kandarian
Keith Lamb
Ron F. Larson D.C.
Craig Lund
Randy McCardle
Gary McLane
Mark Nebeker
Richard L. Nelson Jr.
Ronald H. Norris
Christopher Norris
F. John Parke Jr.
Doug Pinckney
George H. Pinckney Jr.
George H. Pinckney III
Michael W. Riley

Chris Riley
Daniel Riley
Norman Rothman
Bob Rusick
Doug Sallenback
Rob Shockley
Ron Shockley
Keith Stephens
S. Dallas Swenson
Joel Swenson
Merrill Swenson
Ron Swenson
Tei Tanaka
Glen Watson
Glen R. Woodfin

Preface

HOW WE GOT INTO DRESSING MEN

For years in our classes for women, we would hear the lament, "Oh, if only you could help my husband or brother, father, son, boyfriend . . ." and so on. So, in answer to many requests, we offered a color program for men, which soon grew into a six-week wardrobe planning class. A need and interest existed among men as well as women, we had discovered.

But men brought a somewhat different focus to the material, we quickly found. In the six-week class, attendance was sometimes sporadic because many of the men who sought our counsel were off somewhere on business or pleasure every other week. In addition, we consistently heard, "Golly, I wish my wife (or girlfriend) could hear this. She helps me buy my clothes." So we changed our approach: We offered the service as a private consultation and invited the man to bring his wife, best friend, or whomever. That worked better. In our women's classes, we had found that women enjoy watching each other grow, improve and develop as their eight-week session progresses. But men are really not interested in hearing about how to solve other men's clothing problems, only their own. A private session was more efficient. What's more, some of the things that men need to hear—grooming tips, hair and skin care suggestions and the like—are better said in private. The nitty gritty is sometimes a delicate subject, more effectively and comfortably presented in an intimate environment.

You think it's strange that two women are leading fashion consultants for men?

Statistics show that 80% of men's clothing is purchased with or by women—and many women are marvelous at it. The two of us obviously love men: We have dressed two husbands, seven sons and numerous nephews, brothers, in-laws and all their friends.

Men's questions are similar to the ones that women put to us: "Is this my color? Are these shoes my style? Am I the vest type? How about a pinstriped suit? What kind? How should it fit? How many should I have?" The expertise needed to answer these questions is very much like what we needed to know to help the women for whom we had provided guidance for more than 20 years, so helping men was a logical extension of our service.

As our women clients became better dressed, they naturally desired to share their new-found feelings of self-confidence and success with the men in their lives. Meanwhile, the men were finding that good dress and grooming *were* important for their careers and also for their personal and social advancement, but they had never received the training and/or encouragement to become proficient as clothes buyers. It seemed, sometimes, to us that the harder some men had worked to achieve academic, business or professional success, the more negligent they were with their outward appearance. Not because they didn't care, but because they did not have time to develop expertise in this area and did not know where to go for credible assistance in putting together a power-

HOW WE GOT INTO DRESSING MEN

packed wardrobe. Having witnessed the success of their wives and girlfriends, they requested we do the same for them.

The basic principles of color coordination, body typing, fit and personality analysis are much the same as for women. It required several years, however, for us to perfect wardrobe planning for men, gain knowledge of men's hairstyling and grooming, and learn about all the other areas which affected the men we worked with. We gleaned information from the finest tailors, the most reputable sellers of menswear, hairstylists, aestheticians, electrologists, plastic surgeons, and from our men clients themselves.

The information is current and applicable to men in the mainstream of modern life and they flock to hear us at conventions, lectures, seminars and private consultations.

So it was that in 1975, the Fashion Academy Inc. began offering "Executive Grooming For Men." Since that time we have counseled thousands of men from different walks of life—coming from the executive suite to the Hollywood back lot, ranging from college grad to corporate president to retired entrepreneur. We have worked with politicians, ministers, gospel singers, educators, lawyers, entertainers, salesmen, dentists, doctors and engineers.

Men are very logical. You want straight answers and you demand an uncomplicated, workable wardrobe plan. We have yet to meet a man who is not interested in his appearance, though he may profess otherwise; we have yet to work with one who is unwilling to take whatever steps we suggest to achieve the look he wants. It's not hard work—in fact, it's very gratifying when you see just how much of a difference the right styles and colors can mean to your appearance.

Our aim in this book is to lead you step by step through the maze of merchandise and services offered to men today. You will learn to use color most effectively; to analyze your body type in order to purchase becoming, wearable, lasting clothes suited to your lifestyle; to understand how to dress to express your unique personality; and lastly, to put it all together with immaculate grooming, contemporary hair styling and good accessories. You have an idea of how you want your world to see you; here are the rules to help you to project that image.

It is our sincere hope that this book will help you, the reader, accomplish a great look, a planned wardrobe suited to your lifestyle with a maximum of satisfaction and a minimum of cost.

Marge and Gerrie
Fashion Academy
Costa Mesa, California

Clothes make the man. Naked
men have had little or no
influence in society.
                    Mark Twain

The Shades of You

YOUR COLOR PALETTE

Y ou love brown. That should come as no surprise—most men love brown. It is earthy and masculine. Yet you have been told by consultants that you must never be seen in a brown suit—it will ruin your career, your love life and your personality. Poppycock! Most of the surveys and research you have heard reported were done on the East Coast. The ethnic mix in the East, particularly in New York, is predominantly made up of men who don't test well in brown. They don't have the coloring for it, but other men look smashing in brown.

Our intent in this book is to offer you a total wardrobe planning concept so you can present yourself at your best, develop personal style, reduce clothing costs by eliminating mistakes and make this facet of your life more enjoyable.

Color is just one part of the overall picture. Four factors are involved in any outfit you might wear: Its color, the style of the garment, your personality and your lifestyle. While these four are all important, color is by far the most fun, the most intriguing and the first thing people see. Your wardrobe starts with color. The color itself suggests how it can be worn and where it will go, but always remember—the color must harmonize with the man.

COLOR IS THE KEY

You choose your clothing, your accessaccessories, your office decor and sometimes even your car according to your taste in color. Yet men have a particularly difficult time with color. It is reported that one out of every ten men is color blind. We feel that a man's lack of expertise in color stems as much from inadequate training as

from heredity. A boy grows up with his mother choosing his clothes. Later, his girlfriend, wife or a salesperson usually assists him when he goes clothes shopping. The mother, wife or girlfriend may choose colors which she finds pleasing or becoming to herself. The salesperson, of necessity, will choose colors which are in stock. So when does a boy or man learn what goes with what? And what support would he get from his friends if he knew? Young girls are taken shopping by their mothers, often an exciting excursion culminating with a treat at a restaurant. From the teenage years onward, most women use shopping as a major way to socialize as well as to keep up their wardrobes. But boys are rarely taken shopping. If they do go, they prefer a sporting goods store. Boys don't learn to enjoy shopping, and they have little say in the clothing purchased for them. It is debatable whether an innate eye for color fails to develop because it gets no practice or, as the experts suggest, because one in ten men is actually color blind. It is our experience that if we take a pre-school boy shopping, he frequently will choose what is best for him in terms of color, style and personality. Once he starts school, however, he wants only that which his peer group is wearing. Mother goes and buys it, with perhaps more attention to the label than to the color. The result is that generally, regardless of the cause, men usually don't have a very good sense of what colors look best on them or how to coordinate their colors most effectively.

The object of this chapter is to discover which colors are most becoming to your skin tone, eyes and hair. Those of you who feel you do not have a good eye for color or an objective attitude because of preconceived notions might ask for help from your friends or family.

At this point, let's separate clothing choice from home decorating.

The colors you wear are not part of your environment. Once you put them on, you do not see yourself. Colors in a room however, influence you mentally, physically and emotionally. The majority of people will decorate in earth tones because these colors are warm, inviting and cozy. But just because you can live contentedly surrounded by earth tones does not necessarily mean you should wear them. The reverse is also true; many people who look best in the cooler colors like blue could not decorate in those colors because they would freeze to death.

In decorating, you must consider the personalities of those living in the home, the exposure of the room, and the feeling you wish to achieve. You may look terrific in rust, but you may not be able to stand living with it. Blue could be your best color to wear, but it does not necessarily follow that you would want a blue house.

Decorating an office is different. A man should decorate his office in colors which complement him personally and in woods and furniture style which best reflect his personality. His office should create a memorable environment which increases his impact on business associates.

We have found an interesting relationship between the colors that people wear well and their personalities. Colors are usually divided into two undertones: yellow or blue. We have discovered that those who wear the yellow undertones most successfully are often high-key people who may enjoy cooler tones in their environment to calm them down. Conversely, the people who wear blue undertones tend to be more low-key and enjoy warm undertones in their homes to give them a lift.

SEASONS OF COLOR

We have adapted the names and moods of the seasons of the year—Winter, Summer, Spring and Autumn—into a total wardrobe planning concept because colors fall naturally into these groupings. Moreover, this arrangement provides a marvelously effective teaching tool. Each man's skin tone, eyes and hair place him into one of the seasons. Once you know what season you are, you can use the colors of your season's palette to help you plan a wardrobe in which every garment coordinates and is most becoming to you.

The colors are divided first into two groups: Winter and Summer, which have a blue undertone, and Spring and Autumn, which have a yellow undertone.

The colors are then divided again according to their clarity: Winter and Spring are clear, Summer and Autumn are dusty.

The main message of this book is that you can wear any color you wish and look all right, but why should you look just all right when you could look great in colors from your own season's color palette?

We have really not taken anything away from you—there are only five basic primary colors, and you can wear a shade of them all. We are merely guiding you into the proper grouping that will harmonize best with your skin, eyes and hair. You will discover colors in your palette you have never thought of wearing.

We are not trying to change you into something you are not. We *are* trying to lead you into looking your best. Some men have excellent coloring and don't look bad in most colors, but others can't cheat; they can't get away with wearing just any color. Have you ever had someone ask if you were not feeling well? You think, "I felt fine when I got up." But a few comments like that throughout the day, and by evening you are wondering if perhaps you don't feel too well! Your suit could be beautiful, but what is it doing for *you?*

Your best colors are determined by your skin tone. Basically, all those in the same season have the same undertone of skin and will look best in the same undertone of colors.

That Is The Key—Undertone Of The Skin.

We realize that there are some people who can wear colors from more than one season and look okay. But you cannot plan a wardrobe that way, by combining colors from both the yellow and blue undertones. That is why men come to us—they have 10 suits, 25 ties and nothing to wear.

We must give you the discipline of a season to help you develop a well-planned and coordinated wardrobe. This concept provides you with a palette of colors, all of which will be becoming, all of which coordinate.

There is no one who can wear colors from both undertones and of all values and clarity and look equally good in them all. You may think you do, but it is very difficult for you to see yourself objectively. We all have preconceived ideas of what we look like or how we would like to look.

Men usually need to be taught how to use color. For example, it is difficult for a Spring man to imagine his palette in menswear fabrics or for a Winter man to see how his bright colors will integrate into his wardrobe plan.

Did you ever own a suit or an outfit in which you felt really handsome? We suggest that if you will think back to those colors in which you have felt the best and in which you may have received the most compliments, you might have a clue as to which colors are best for you.

WHAT DETERMINES YOUR SEASON?

Your season is determined by your skin, your eyes and your hair. Skin is the most important; next the eyes, and then the hair. Your season cannot be determined by just one of these three, especially the eyes, because so many variations of eye color occur from one season to another. We

must consider all three in the final analysis. Nature coordinated all three to go together. We have never seen a man whose skin, eyes and hair did not go well together.

SKIN

Just as we find cool and warm undertones in colors, we find cool and warm undertones in skin. All skin has a blue undertone with a purple base, or it has a yellow undertone with a green base. The basic undertone does not change, although it may fade with age. You may tan or freckle, but people tan different shades depending on their skin tone. Some people have good natural coloring, others are sallow. Wearing the right colors will make blemishes appear to fade, make wrinkles less noticeable and enhance your natural skin tone. Various conditions can affect the outward appearance of your skin: Illness, fatigue, diet (carrots and acidic foods and juices), use of tobacco or alcohol, an extreme suntan or improperly dyed hair may all contribute.

EYES

Your eye color usually changes from birth to childhood and again in maturity. The normal pattern is that you are born with dark blue eyes, which then change to a color which later fades with age. Your eyes are usually darker, brighter and more clear in youth than they are in maturity. We have found that blue-eyed people have more pink in their skin, while brown-eyed people tend to be more sallow.

HAIR

Your hair complements your skin tone. It may have as many as seven different shades. Hair color changes with age—you may have been born with dark hair, then it turned blond, later it went medium or dark and then turned gray. No matter what your natural hair color, what we are trying to

YOUR COLOR PALETTE

create is a harmony between your skin, your eyes, your hair and your clothing. If you touch up your hair, you should choose a color on the hair color chart which is one or two shades lighter than your natural hair, or the result will be too dark.

THE MUNSELL COLOR THEORY

At the Fashion Academy we have based our color concept on a color theory established by Albert H. Munsell, the greatest American colorist. Munsell's work is classical. It established permanent values in the art and science of color. His theory is considered the most logical and understandable in existence. Accepted by the U.S. Department of Agriculture and the *Encyclopedia Britannica*, it is used by most artists, dress designers, interior decorators and architects.

Munsell's theory is based on five *basic primary colors: red, yellow, green, blue and purple*. Munsell eliminated orange from his primary palette because he felt the inclusion of orange resulted in an unbalanced color wheel with too much yellow. We agree, because we have also found that yellow is the least becoming color on most people. You will note that we have eliminated orange from the Winter and Summer palettes. From Munsell's five basic hues are produced all the intermediate colors. Your selection of becoming colors is almost unlimited as long as you remember a few basic rules: *Everyone can wear all five of these basic primary colors depending on the undertone, the value and the clarity of a color.*

Before we go on to discuss the role of color in fashion, let us define a few terms:

Hue means color. It is the quality which distinguishes one color from another—for example, red from blue.

Undertone describes the color you get when you take the five basic hues and add either blue or yellow to them. For example, undertones can be a blue-red or a yellow-red, a blue-green or a yellow-green.

Value is the quality of lightness or darkness found in a color. It differentiates a light blue from a dark blue, for example, or a light pink from a maroon.

Clarity or *Chroma* is the quality of brightness or dullness of a color. Compare a fresh new leaf, strong and bright in color, to the same leaf in the autumn—dull and dusty. Contrast a clear pink to a muted, dusty pink.

Winters wear the true basic primary hues and the five hues with blue added to them. Winter colors, whether true or blue, are clear. You can wear all of your colors in values from icy light to almost black. Winter is the only season whose coloring is strong enough to wear black and chalk white successfully.

Summers wear the five basic primary hues with blue added to them. Their colors are most becoming when they are muted or dusty. You can wear medium to light values of your colors either clear or muted, but any hue which is medium to dark in value must be muted.

Springs wear the five basic primary hues with yellow added. Their colors are clear. Springs look best in shades which are medium to light in value. The darker colors are too strong for their coloring. Your suits may be closer to Autumn because menswear fabrics are usually of muted colors. Just be certain that your shirt and tie are in your clear shades.

Autumns wear the five basic primary hues with yellow added and they are muted or dusty. Many of Autumn's colors overlap with Spring, especially in your browns and golds. It is much easier for an Autumn to borrow the clear colors of Spring than for Spring to borrow the dusty shades of Autumn. The Autumn man can successfully borrow Spring's yellow undertoned hues which are clear and *bright*, but not those which are clear and *light*. You should also avoid the blues and pinks of the Spring palette.

Five Basic Primary Colors

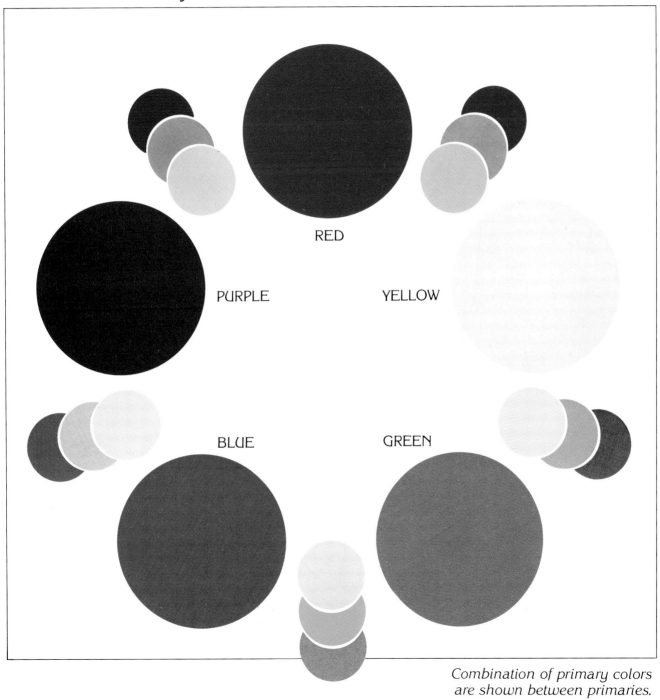

RED

PURPLE   YELLOW

BLUE   GREEN

*Combination of primary colors
are shown between primaries.*

THE SHADES OF YOU

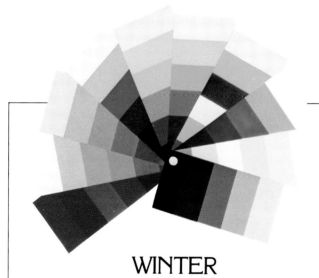

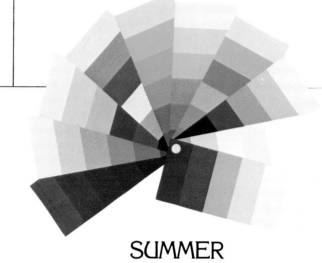

WINTER

SUMMER

Doug
Typical Winter

Gary
Typical Summer

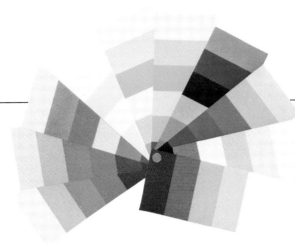

SPRING

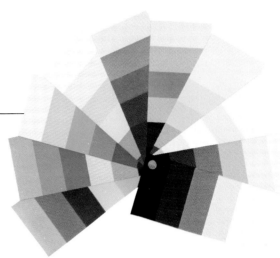

AUTUMN

Keith
Typical Spring

Tim
Typical Autumn

THE SHADES OF YOU

Ron
Fair white skin, deep blue-gray eyes,
brown-black hair.

Joel
Olive skin, olive-brown eyes,
chestnut brown hair.

Gabe
Dark olive skin, dark brown eyes,
black hair.

Tei
Olive skin, dark brown eyes, black hair,
silver-gray at temples.

WINTER SEASON

Richard
Dark brown-black skin, dark
brown-black eyes, black hair.

Bob
Deep rose-beige skin, brown eyes,
salt and pepper hair.

WINTER PALETTE

The Winter man wears the true basic primary colors. He also wears the true basic primary colors with blue added to them. The Winter can wear all values of the primary colors from light to dark, but the intensity must be clear, not dusty. Winter and Summer are cousins because their colors are of a blue undertone. Some of their colors will overlap. The key to the Winter color selection is: True or Blue and Clear. Winters wear silver jewelry which harmonizes with their skin and colors.

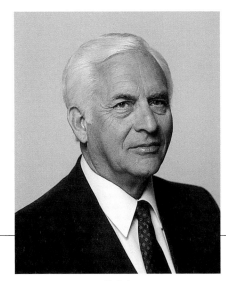

Ralph
Olive skin, blue-gray eyes,
silver-gray hair.

THE SHADES OF YOU

SUMMER SEASON

Rob
Fair pink skin, blue-gray eyes,
light ash blonde hair.

Gary
Rose-beige skin, blue eyes,
ash brown hair.

Kevin
Rosy-pink skin, clear blue eyes,
medium ash blonde hair.

Mickey
Rose-beige skin, light blue eyes,
light ash brown hair.

SUMMER SEASON

Ned
Deep rose-beige skin, deep blue eyes, dark
ash brown hair, silver gray at temples.

John
Rose-beige skin, aqua-blue eyes,
ash gray hair.

SUMMER PALETTE

The Summer man wears dusty, muted shades
of blue or rose overtones. When colors are
medium to light, they can be dusty or clear, but
when they are from medium to dark, they should
be dusty. Dark, bright, intense colors wil overpower
the Summer man. The key to the Summer color
selection is: Blue undertones of soft pastels to
dusty dark tones. Summer men wear silver jewelry.

Ron
Rose-beige skin, light clear blue eyes,
silver-gray hair.

THE SHADES OF YOU

Ken
Peach-pink skin, deep blue eyes,
golden blonde hair.

Dallas
Warm beige skin, clear blue eyes,
medium warm brown hair.

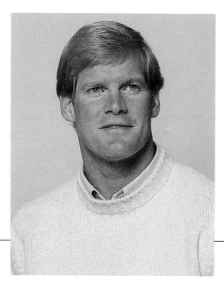

Mark
Fair peach-pink, ruddy skin, light
aqua-blue eyes, carrot red hair.

Reed
Peach skin, medium blue eyes,
light warm brown hair.

SPRING SEASON

Webb
Warm golden beige skin, blue-green
eyes, strawberry blonde hair.

Doug
Warm golden skin, blue-green eyes
medium warm brown hair.

SPRING PALETTE

The Spring man wears yellow undertones —warm, clear, fresh-fruit, spring bouquet colors. Spring has the greatest range of colors of any season. His only limitation is that he cannot successfully wear colors which are very dark. The key to the Spring color selection is: Yellow undertone, clear, medium to light colors. The Spring man wears gold jewelry.

Merrill
Pale ivory skin, light
blue eyes, warm white hair.

THE SHADES OF YOU

AUTUMN SEASON

Craig
Deep beige skin, dark brown eyes,
medium golden brown hair.

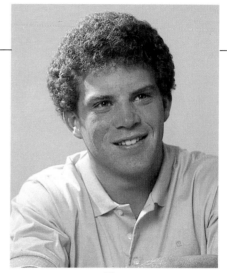

Troy
Peach-pink, ruddy skin, olive-brown
eyes, bright red hair.

Glen
Golden beige skin, golden brown
eyes, dark blonde hair (dishwater).

Tim
Warm beige skin, green-brown eyes,
warm brown hair.

AUTUMN SEASON

Ron
Beige skin, green-brown eyes, medium
brown hair, streaked with gray.

Buddy
Golden beige skin with freckles, rich
brown eyes, red-brown hair now graying.

AUTUMN PALETTE

The Autumn man wears yellow undertones, earthy muted shades and colors of metal and wood. Spring and Autumn are cousins. A few of their warm clear colors will overlap, especially in yellows, oranges and browns. The key to Autumn color selection is: Yellow undertone, dusty, muted, earth tones. The Autumn man wears gold jewelry.

Ron
Fair, ruddy skin, blue-green
(turquoise) eyes, auburn hair.

Ron
An Autumn

When hair is graying it must be well styled and perfectly groomed. The right colors and a good hair cut made Ron look twenty years younger.

Jim
A Spring

A handsome young man, he was disguising his vibrant youthfulness with a scraggly beard, a too-thin moustache and neglected hair.

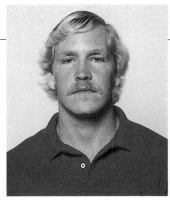

Keith
A Spring

Keith needed his hair shaped at the top, trimmed off his neck and blow-dried to balance a broad jawline. He needs to keep his moustache neatly trimmed above the corners of his mouth. A subtle assist changed him from ordinary to handsome.

Marge and Gerrie
consulting with client.

AREAS OF CRITICAL FIT

BACK OF PANTS

PANT LENGTH

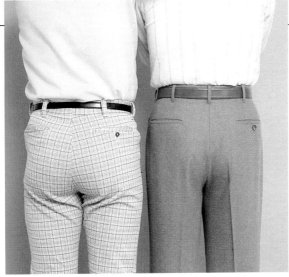

Wrong
This graphic example shows drag lines under the buttocks, pulling towards the inseam. Center back seam is too deep causing wrinkles under the buttocks.

Right
The smooth, straight hang of these pants indicates that the center back seam is near to straight of grain. Fabric which hangs on grain eliminates most wrinkles under the buttocks and drag lines towards inseam.

Wrong
Skimpy, tapered pant legs cause the bottom of pants to ride too high on the instep. The resulting shorter pant makes the legs appear shorter and the feet look bigger.

Right
Straight or slightly shaped pants hit the foot at the toe of the shoe and can be hemmed longer at the heel. This visually lengthens the legs and makes the feet appear to be in better proportion.

SIZING OF SUITS

Wrong
This suit is too wide in the shoulders. The jacket and sleeves are too long and the sleeve is too full. The excess fabric is in front of the arm, creating drag lines which point towards the back of the sleeve. A suit too big or too long makes a man appear older, shorter and heavier.

Right
This suit fits snug in the shoulders. The jacket comes barely to the crotch which lengthens the leg. The sleeve is in good proportion to the body with a high armseye. Snug fit in a suit makes a man appear younger, slimmer, taller and more affluent.

Upper Back

The upper back of the suit coat should fit smoothly, with only a moderate amount of excess fabric on each side. Approximately 1/2 inch of the shirt collar should show above the suit collar in back.

Sleeves

The arms should be in the middle of the sleeves with approximately the same amount of room in front and in back. The fabric near the top of the sleeves should be smooth, with the flesh of the upper arms immediately under the fabric.

Lapels

The suit lapel should snug into the body and cover the bottom of the shirt collar on the side front. The suit lapel should ride close to the body and not gap over the chest.

THE SHADES OF YOU

Chris   Mike   Daniel

Mike and his two sons were all born with dark hair which then turned light ash-blonde like Daniel's, then medium brown like Chris. Both children will be dark like their father when they are grown. Mike, the father, is turning prematurely gray. This is a typical Winter pattern. All three have rose-beige skin and blue-gray eyes.

Ron and his son, Christopher were born dark, then turned tow heads. With maturity the hair turns very dark brown. Ron and Christopher have fair white skin and deep blue-gray eyes.

Christopher   Ron

Your exercise in self-discovery can be an interesting experience. It will require objectivity, honesty and a good memory of your childhood coloring. Keep in mind your skin coloring without a tan, your eye color both as a child and as an adult, your hair color as a child and as a young man, and your *true* hair color as an adult. This could be a little difficult for those of you who have very little hair or none at all, but do the best you can.

Read the descriptions that follow of all four seasons. Which coloring and inner season most nearly describe you, and which group of colors have you most enjoyed wearing?

THE WINTER MAN

There are more Winters in the world than individuals of any other season because there are more dark people. Because of mixed racial heritages, Winters can come from any nationality. Southern European and South American people are usually Winters with light to dark olive skin. The dark Irish and Welsh are often Winters with their striking contrast of light skin and dark hair. American Indians are Winters with dark red-brown or yellow-brown skin. No doubt it was the red-brown shade of skin which led to Indians being called "redskins." The Polynesians and people of Eastern Asia and India are Winters with skin ranging from olive-brown to black.

All Orientals are Winters. Depending on their heredity, their skin coloring can range from porcelain white to dark yellow-brown.

The Winter season takes in all blacks, even though they, like Orientals, may be of different shades depending on their heredity. The very dark-blue black man can probably wear any season's colors, but we put him in the Winter season because he looks best in its clear strong hues, and the designation gives him discipline in wardrobe planning. The light to dark-brown blacks should never wear warm, muted Autumn shades because those colors turn their skins sallow.

Winter Skin

The Winter man has a blue undertone with a purple base in his skin. Light to dark olive is the most common of the Winter skin tones, but it is also the hardest in which to detect the blue undertone because the skin is usually thicker, causing it to look yellow. The blue undertone of the skin, influenced by the yellow overtone, produces a grayish cast. This is especially noticeable when the olive-skinned person is tired or ill. Do not confuse olive skin with yellow-beige skin which has a green base, as found in the Autumn-Spring people. If you put yellow-undertone colors on olive skin, that skin will look very yellow, sallow and tired. But by putting blue-undertoned colors on olive skin, you will bring out the purple base, making the skin look more rosy, healthy and alive.

The darker the skin, as with blacks, the more noticeable the blue undertone. The yellow overcast is more noticeable in brown-skinned people, because it makes them appear sallow.

Most Winters tan easily, while some don't tan at all. Others freckle. This is due to the red pigment in their skin. The tan of a Winter is usually a reddish-brown tan and can look dirty if he gets too dark.

Winters are prone to dark circles under the eyes. Due to the purple base, their eyelids and lips take on a blue-red cast.

YOUR COLOR PALETTE

Winter Skin Tones:
☐ White
☐ Light to deep rose-beige
☐ Light to dark olive
☐ Brown
☐ Brown-black
☐ Black

Winter Eyes

All eye colors can be found in the Winter season, but brown is predominant. Brown eyes might range from a very light golden-brown, to a medium olive-brown, to a dark brown, to a black-brown. Often in the brown-eyed Winter you will see a violet tint around his pupils and a gray ring around his irises. You may see gold and/or green flecks in the light to medium brown eyes. Blue eyes found in Winter usually have gray in them. Some blue eyes contain light flecks which look like granite or slate. When the eye is blue, you will generally find more pink in the skin. Green eyes found in Winter are usually a clear gray-green or green with gold flecks, which could be mistaken for olive-green eyes found in Autumn. These green eyes often have a gray ring around the irises. Turquoise eyes, a blue-green combination often with a grayish cast, are found in Winter as well. Winter hazel eyes have a combination of blue, green and brown, with the blue or green found more toward the outside of the irises and the brown stronger near the pupils. Some Winters have eyes resembling a German brown trout with dark brown-black and gold flecks.

Infrequent combinations found in Winter are eyes resembling a light blue or green transparent marble and deep royal blue eyes with violet rings shading into the blue irises around the pupils, which give the impression of being violet eyes. These eyes can look blue or violet, depending on the colors worn or the mood of the person.

Those who have from light to deep rose-beige skin usually will have a blue or gray shade in their eyes. Brown- or hazel-eyed

Winters are usually more sallow, which would indicate that less blue is coming through in the skin. This could trick you into thinking that you are a yellow-beige-skinned Autumn.

Winter Eyes Are:
☐ Light to dark brown
☐ Black-brown
☐ Blue-gray
☐ Gray-green
☐ Green-gold (olive-green)
☐ Turquoise
☐ Dark Blue-violet
☐ Hazel

Winter Hair

Some Winters may have been towheads as children, others golden honey blonds who turned dark with maturity. Winters rarely stay blond as adults; moreover, they will often gray prematurely. The darker the hair, the more gracefully it grays. When Winters turn gray, it is a silver-gray. However, through the effects of exposure to the sun, hair sprays, shampoos or excessive smoking, their hair may acquire a yellow tinge. Winters should protect their hair from the sun. Light to medium to dark brown Winter hair will present a cool quality, although young people with cool brown hair might appear to have warm brown hair because they have overexposed it to the sun and bleached the ends. It can even appear to have auburn highlights. The sunbleached Winter's true hair color can be determined at the roots on the back of the head, near the neck. This same type of hair will often turn very dark with maturity when it is no longer exposed to so much sunlight.

Winters with dark brown hair will typically turn quite dark just before turning gray.

Many Winters have chestnut brown hair which has red highlights in it, especially in warmer climates where the hair is exposed to sun bleaching. Those natural red highlights are more of a copper-red than an orange-red. Many dark-haired, olive-skinned Winter men will have red sideburns and a red beard. The gray-haired Winter man should protect his hair from sunlight, because the sun will give his silver-gray hair a yellow cast.

Winter Hair Is:
☐ Platinum blond or golden-blonde or brown (on young men)
☐ Medium to dark brown
☐ Chestnut brown
☐ Black-brown or black
☐ Gray (silver)

Your Inner Season

Over the years, we have noticed similarities between people of the same season in the ways they act and look at life. We make no assertion that our conclusions are scientific. Our comments on the "inner season" are all in fun—but they can be uncanny in accuracy. Your inner season has nothing to do with astrology; it is neither mysterious nor mystical. The comments are based solely on our pleasant association with and observations of men.

The Winter man is distinct and definite, a realist with an air of sophistication. His independence may make him appear aloof, but he has an inner warmth and radiates a strong, masculine and highly individual charm. He has a magnetic appeal to women. Cool, logical, adventurous and determined, the Winter man often possesses a methodical mind and is skilled with his hands. He has a will of iron and is sometimes stubborn, domineering and aggressive. A believer in and user of the positive approach, he is serenely confident and retains his composure in a crisis. His emotional attachments are permanent. He never vacillates, is rarely impulsive, is a strong leader and likes things done his way. He presents a facade of self-assurance at all times. The Winter man is not quick to anger, but he never forgets. He has few intimate friends but is admired and highly respected by his peers. Ambitious, hardworking, and intelligently organized, he likes to plan his life in detail.

It is important for the Winter man to understand the effect he has on other people. His darkness makes him less approachable; therefore, a Winter usually must make the overtures of friendship, be the first to smile and extend a cordial greeting. The Winter man must be particularly supportive of acquaintances, friends and especially employees over whom he might have authority. His positive approach, decisiveness and strong leadership can be frightening, especially if he is aggressive.

A Winter's path through life will be smoother if he can learn to soften his approach. He must recognize that by just standing there, he can intimidate other people.

Prototypes: Christopher Reeves, Jack Klugman, Telly Savalas, Muhammed Ali, Eric Estrada, Dustin Hoffman, Tom Selleck.

THE SUMMER MAN

Summer men display a classic reserve and an even temperament. The Summer season combines racial mixtures—many are found with a heritage from the British Isles, the Scandinavian countries, the Netherlands or Northern European countries. Fewer Summers turn up among our clients than people of the other seasons. We do not necessarily feel that there are fewer Summers among the population, but we do attest to the fact that a Summer is less inclined to spend time or money for this type of course for himself. He would freely give it to his wife or daughter, however. If we can once convince a Summer that he can develop his full potential by utilizing the things we teach, he becomes our most devoted fan and faithful convert.

YOUR COLOR PALETTE

An interesting note: We have found in our travels around the country that many other color consultants, due perhaps to a poor eye for color or lack of training, assign many people who are not Summers into this season.

Summer Skin

Summer skin has a blue undertone which gives it a pink, rosy cast.

Summers seem to have thin skins. They often flush easily, and when they blush, the color is instant. Summers with deeper rose-beige skin—those closer to the Winter season—will tan more easily than the rest, and their tan will be a red-brown. But most Summers do not tan well, they burn and peel. By nature, Summers are not sun worshipers. They tend to protect themselves from the sun. There are a few Summers who may appear sallow or gray, which could be due to poor health.

Summer Skin Is:
☐ Fair with delicate pink tone
☐ Light to medium rose-beige
☐ Deep rose-beige

Summer Eyes

Summer eyes can range from clear blue or green to gray-blue, gray-green, aqua-marine, hazel or brown. Blue is the most common eye color for a Summer. Few brown eyes are found in the Summer man; those brown eyes we do see are a soft brown. The Summer blue eyes can be a very clear blue, almost like a marble; others are a deep blue-gray with a violet tint around the pupils and a gray ring around the irises, much like Winter eyes. Green eyes found in Summer can be clear green to a gray-green with soft white or yellow radiating out from the pupils.

Hazel eyes of a Summer are a blue-green with brown and/or yellow flecks. These eyes have a chameleon-like quality of changing color depending on the Summer man's mood or on what color he's wearing.

Summer Eyes Are:
☐ Clear blue or gray-blue
☐ Clear green or gray-green
☐ Aquamarine
☐ Hazel
☐ Soft, cool brown

Summer Hair

Some Summers have very light ash blond hair which often darkens with age. This type is a true blond. Many Summers were towheads as children. The light to dark brown hair of this season appears to be a mousy color because of its grayish cast. This hair may appear dull and lifeless when the wrong colors are worn, but it looks very attractive when enhanced by the right colors.

Summer men gray gracefully, turning a silver gray. Many fair Summers with light hair will grow dark beards. Summers whose skin coloring is high, or pink, have a lot of red pigment which will bring out red highlights in their hair when it is exposed to sunlight.

Summer Hair Is:
☐ Light ash blond
☐ Medium ash blond
☐ Light to medium ash brown
☐ Dark ash brown
☐ Gray

Your Inner Season

The Summer man is the Classic type with a gentle masculinity. He is gracious, poised, and inspires confidence in women. Even-tempered, he has a calm voice. Getting more done with less effort, he is artistic and excels in many endeavors. The Summer man is a good listener and is very interested in other people. There is a stubborn side to him, too—he is quite set in his ways and at times may prove hard to convince. He is fun but never fickle. He is a good sport, a loyal friend, a devoted husband and family man. Secure in his own home, the Summer man is happy playing the role of a father, and he often gets involved in school and community volunteer work. The Summer man is the salt of the earth and the backbone of the nation.

The Summer man is a fashion conservative. His classic gentility is expressed in muted colors. He should never attempt a dramatic or extreme effect. He has a comfort zone and is not eager to step out of it. Slow to consider a new fashion, he is usually the last to adopt it and by the time he does, it is almost out of style. His wife and children always get new shoes; if there is any money left in the budget, he might get around to buying himself a pair. The Summer man is a bit of a penny-pincher who would rather spend his money on tools or hobbies than on himself.

Prototypes: Johnny Carson, Paul Newman, Phil Donahue, Merv Griffin, James Stewart.

THE SPRING MAN

The typical Spring man has an "All-American," boy-next-door, golden look that comes about in part from the yellow undertone in his skin. Many Spring men are descendants of the Scandinavian races, or people of the Netherlands, British Isles, Iceland and Northern Europe. Springs take great interest in the course at the Fashion Academy because they are very interested in personal appearance, their own and everybody else's. They are delightful and enthusiastic men to have around. We always get a lift out of Springs. They are so eager to learn that they want the whole course in the first five minutes.

Spring Skin

Ivory with gold-tone skin is typical of individuals in the Spring season. Some are so fair that they appear milky white, even sickly, with skin and hair the same color. Their pink or peach skin has a glow to it with rosy cheeks. Springs may flush easily and have almost a redheaded ruddiness. Some Springs will freckle. A deep-peach-skinned Spring tans very easily and, if an outdoor man, will hold the tan all year. Light to medium beige skin has more yellow in it and looks sallow. This coloring is closest to Autumn.

Spring Skin Tones:
☐ Pale ivory
☐ Golden ivory
☐ Pink or peach
☐ Deep peach
☐ Light to medium beige
☐ Ruddy

Spring Eyes

All eye colors are found in Spring, though there seem to be more blue and fewer brown. Spring eyes range from light to dark blue. Some Springs have blue-gray eyes that may have a gray ring around the irises and a mixture of gold and white flecks resembling granite around the pupils. Many Springs have aqua, or green-blue, eyes with gold flecks. Topaz, a golden yellow, is a beautiful and unusual eye color found in Spring, while golden-green eyes are very common among Spring men. There are few brown eyes, and those few found in Spring are light brown with gold and/or green flecks. Hazel eyes found in Spring are blue-green with some brown radiating from the pupils.

Spring Eyes Are:
☐ Light to dark blue
☐ Blue-gray
☐ Green-blue (aqua)
☐ Gold-green
☐ Light gold-brown
☐ Topaz-yellow
☐ Hazel

YOUR COLOR PALETTE

Spring Hair

Springs are most often blond, their hair color ranging from a light flaxen to a golden honey or light to medium brown with gold highlights. Spring blonds usually darken with age, but the sun keeps their hair light in the summer. Some fair Springs may have had bright carrot-red hair as babies or children; with maturity this hair will usually turn to a strawberry blond or a golden honey brown. Spring men may have red beards and sideburns. They could also grow very dark beards.

A few Springs with blond or brown hair have red highlights. Some Springs' brown hair appears darker during the winter months and lightens very quickly when exposed to the sun in the summer months.

Many Springs do not gray gracefully, because the gray tones in their light hair often give it a drab look. When completely gray, their hair is a soft white-gray.

Spring Hair Is:
☐ Flaxen blond
☐ Golden blond
☐ Strawberry blond
☐ Light to dark golden brown
☐ Gray
☐ White (warm)

Your Inner Season

The Spring man is exciting, unpredictable, and fun to have around. He'll never go to bed early if there is anything interesting happening, and on occasion, he loves to sleep late. An extrovert whose gregarious facade often disguises his true nature, he is sometimes shy but enjoys being in the limelight. Possessed of a mercurial disposition, the Spring man may sulk if he doesn't get his way; his temper may erupt quickly but just as rapidly subside. Financial security is important to him. He has many plans but may be distracted before he follows through. Ready to go at a moment's notice, he is impulsive, friendly, smiles easily, moves quickly, is informally hospitable, and loves luxury. He is proficient at hobbies or home repair but rarely puts his tools away. His appearance is important to him. Energetic and fun-loving, the Spring man has a warm heart, and many friends. He makes a super salesman and people motivator. While he loves children and pets, he is happy to allow someone else to care for them. He may not appear to be studious, but never underestimate his intelligence. He may appear innocent and naive, but he knows what he is doing every minute. The Spring man is ageless, with a clean-cut, wholesome, natural appeal.

Prototypes: John Davidson, Ron Howard, Morgan Stevens, Ryan O'Neal, Johnny Miller.

THE AUTUMN MAN

Autumns can be a blend of any racial background with no specific origin, unless you count the redheaded Irish. We have fewer Autumns than people of other seasons at the Academy because they are too busy to take time out for classes. Autumns always have a lot of irons in the fire.

Autumns have a yellow undertone to their skin, and many of them appear sallow. Most redheads are Autumns unless they have blue eyes, and then they are probably Springs. Autumns have light brows and lashes, and they lack much natural color in their lips and cheeks. Most look best with a little tan on their faces to add color. When an Autumn is sick he looks sick, almost green. Many men, especially Winters, think that they are Autumns because they like brown, and have worn camel and beige-- two classic Autumn colors. But in order to be an Autumn you must be able to wear all of the dusty greens, rusts, yellows and golds as well.

Autumn Skin

Some Autumns have very fair ivory skin which does not tan easily. Others have peach skin, ranging from light to deep. This skin has more color and may look ruddy or florid. Any of the lighter Autumn skin tones may freckle. The beige skin, light to dark, is very sallow and its yellow undertone is more noticeable. Medium to deep beige skin tans more easily. Autumns usually tan a golden color, but the deeper beige skin when very tan can look dirty.

Autumn Skin Tones:
☐ Ivory
☐ Light, medium or deep peach
☐ Light, medium or dark beige
☐ Ruddy

Autumn Eyes

Most Autumns have brown eyes, but "brown" can cover a wide spectrum—from golden amber with dark brown or black flecks, to light to dark reddish-brown with a rich rust color circling the pupils and fading out into the darker brown of the outer irises.

Many Autumn children have very dark brown eyes, almost black-looking, but with maturity their eyes may lighten. Eyes which were brown in youth often mature with green in them or look hazel.

Autumns may have avocado-green eyes with gold flecks—known as cat eyes—or olive-green or olive-brown eyes.

The Autumn man's hazel eyes will be predominantly brown with a little blue-green in them.

There are very few blue eyes found in Autumn. The eyes may be turquoise, but they will be more green than blue.

Autumn's eyes are truly the windows of his soul. His eyes are very expressive and change with his mood. When Autumns are happy or excited, their eyes sparkle and dance. The flecks of gold make them shine.

Autumn Eyes Are:
☐ Light to dark brown, red-brown, olive-brown
☐ Golden-green (cat eyes)
☐ Hazel
☐ Turquoise

AUTUMN HAIR

Most Autumn children have golden honey blond to light brown hair which will darken with age.

Autumns may have honey blond to golden blond to dishwater blond hair. The dishwater blond is really a drab brown with gold highlights. You will often see this color hair on young men. On some it appears dull, but on others it may be bright and shiny.

Autumns might also have strawberry blond or light to medium sandy-red hair; or they may be bright carrot-tops or deep auburn. Red hair is most predominant in the Autumn season, and most Autumns look good with red highlights in their hair. The sun often brings that red out.

Light to dark brown hair may have gold or red highlights. The dark brown hair may be a deep chestnut with auburn highlights. Autumns do not gray gracefully. Their transition period of graying is not attractive until they are completely gray because the gray mixed with their warm highlights gives their hair a dull, drab look. Their gray hair is a warm gray. When an Autumn man goes gray, his skin and eyes also fade somewhat, leaving little contrast between hair and face. The lack of color contrast can be aging. For this reason, we never hesitate to encourage a graying Autumn man to use a color rinse on his hair.

If an Autumn man should ever want to color his hair, he should use a solid color with red or gold highlights. Your hairdresser can provide the professional advice you need. If your hair is just starting to turn gray but your beard has obvious gray patches, reconsider wearing facial hair because it will be aging at this period of your life.

YOUR COLOR PALETTE

Autumn Hair Is:
☐ Honey blond
☐ Strawberry blond
☐ Bright red to deep auburn
☐ Light to dark brown
  with gold or red highlights
☐ Deep chestnut-brown
☐ Gray
☐ White (warm)

Your Inner Season

The Autumn man is busy and colorful. He is most often an extrovert, but at times may be quiet and reserved; he is subject to extremes of temperament, very high or very low. While quick to fly off the handle, he is fast to forgive and forget. The Autumn male has independence, originality of thought, a positive voice, and a firm step. Capable of leadership, he knows his own mind and is quick in making decisions. He is annoyed when other people disrupt his sense of organization by carelessly using his things.

Loyal and affectionate, the Autumn man is inventive, courageous, and an incurable optimist. He has a keen sense of humor. He is also sensitive, temperamental, mischievous, willful, and proud. While he is patient, he will retaliate if you push him too far. He moves quickly, smiles easily, is friendly and impulsive. Thriving on luxury, he loves the spotlight. The Autumn man is artistic and creative, a stimulating and sought-after friend but a very private person.

Prototypes: Prince Charles, Robert Redford, Charlton Heston.

Whatever season you are, you will enhance your appearance by wearing those colors that are best for you.

Those of you who may have difficulty in determining your season might benefit from the assistance of a trained and certified Fashion Academy Consultant.

Once your season has been determined, it is time to look at your next dimension, your body type, to see how it affects your clothing choices.

Body Works   2

Whenever you shop for your clothes, you face a potential problem with the ready-to-wear fashions available to you. The prices may be reasonable, the selection stylish and the whole shopping process relatively convenient, but the clothes themselves may not fit right.

In dealing with ready-to-wear, you come face to face with the proportions of the hypothetical "norm" or "AVERAGE" male figure as the manufacturers conceive it to be. Before you can consider style or design, you must discover how you will fit into the clothing available to you.

What you are trying to do with clothing is to achieve the illusion of what is currently considered to be a perfectly proportioned male body. The concept of perfection changes from decade to decade. People in our society today have been conditioned— consciously or subconsciously—to admire the tall, lean figure with broad shoulders, slim hips and long legs. This is due partly to the actual dimensions of the human figure, partly to the fashion media and partly to current enthusiasm for athletic slimness.

If you divide your body at the point where your legs attach to your torso, you will find that your legs are an inch or two longer than your upper body. The eye, therefore, is accustomed to long legs. In addition, for the past thirty years the fashion media have presented the stylish figure with extremely long legs, often comprising as much as two-thirds of the body length. For three decades, then, your eye has been conditioned to find this silhouette pleasing. Thus, part of your effort in choosing your clothing is to create an illusion of long legs. If you can visually lengthen the legs, you can make your body appear to be in better proportion—taller, younger, slimmer and more fashionable.

To see how this information on fashion line applies to ready-to-wear, we must go back to the clothing manufacturer. Every garment manufacturer has a master pattern from which he cuts his clothing. This master pattern incorporates the manufacturer's perception of how his customer is proportioned. Traditionally, these proportions did not vary much from one manufacturer or cutter to the next. But in the past few years, cutters started clinging less to the basic norm and began to show an awareness of the varying shapes of men. Your challenge is to find the manufacturer who has *you* in mind when he makes his clothes.

While we have never seen a perfectly proportioned man, there must be one somewhere. Many men come close to the ideal, but most have figures which vary somewhat from the so-called average or norm. These variations, while not detracting from a man's general appearance, might make it difficult for him to fit properly into ready-to-wear garments.

ANALYSIS OF PHYSIQUE AND POSTURE

READY-TO-WEAR IS USUALLY CONSTRUCTED WITH THESE GENERAL PROPORTIONS IN MIND

Remember the young men in pictures posted on a gym wall or the handsome male models in a store catalog? Cutters design clothing to hang on this type of posture. Strive to achieve and maintain good posture and a vital and alert attitude. The primary indications of old age are poor posture and slow movement.

The fit of your clothes depends primarily on your posture. If fitting were merely a matter of girth, manufacturers could simply allow big seams that could be let out or taken in to fit any size body. Fit—particularly the hang of jackets or coats and the drape of pants—is greatly influenced by the way you stand. For instance, a man whose head is set forward will have collars and ties that bind in front and a horizontal wrinkle that runs across the front of his shirts and sweaters.

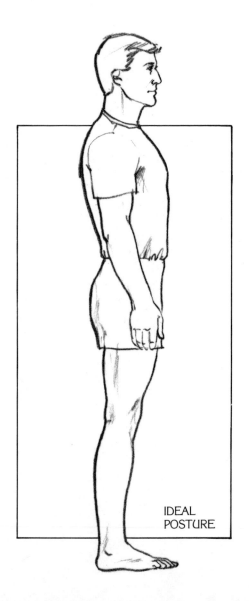

IDEAL
POSTURE

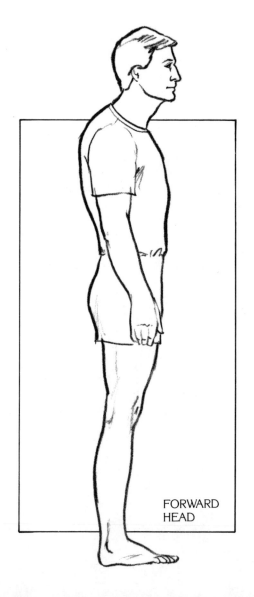

FORWARD
HEAD

The man who stands with his shoulders hunched forward, causing a more rounded back than average, will find that his suit coats appear to be shorter in the back.

Someone with very erect posture, on the other hand, will have a wrinkle running horizontally across his suit just above the waistline in back.

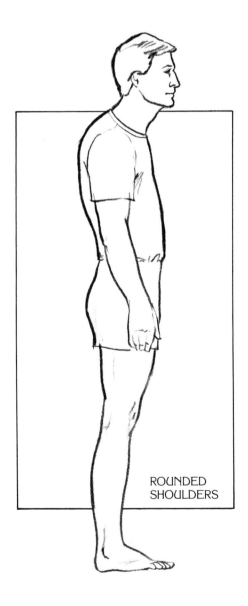

ROUNDED
SHOULDERS

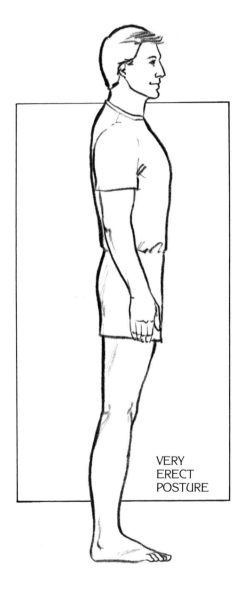

VERY
ERECT
POSTURE

ANALYSIS OF PHYSIQUE AND POSTURE

Ideally, the arm of a person's body rides in the middle of a jacket sleeve with the same amount of room in front and in back of the arm. The sleeve should hang smoothly, with the threads across the cap running approximately parallel to the floor.

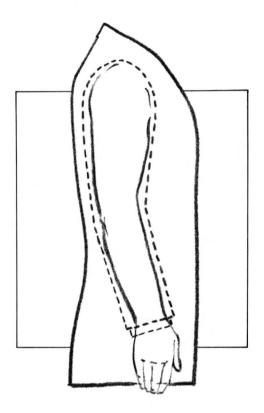

Most cutters of pants assume that a man's rump sticks out in back. Thus, men who have flat bottoms or who tuck their buttocks under will often find that their pants wrinkle under the buttocks. A man with full, muscular calves or one who locks his knees has a hyper-extended calf, and he will find that his slacks do not hang smoothly from the seat to the hem.

Cutters assume that all men's bodies have a two-inch drop from the base of the neck to the tip of the shoulder. If your shoulders are more square than that norm, they will literally lift your suit at the tip of the shoulders, creating excess fabric just below the collarline in back. This is the single most common flaw in men's ready-to-wear clothing. The situation raises a very logical question: "Why don't cutters do some research to find out whether more consumers might benefit if shoulders were made more square—by perhaps one-quarter to one-half inch?"

A very square-shouldered man will invariably have gaping suit lapels, horizontal shirt wrinkles running diagonally toward the tip of each shoulder, and the inevitable excess fabric below suit and jacket collars in back.

A man whose shoulders slope more than the two-inch norm is more unusual. This man will find that his suit rides on his body at the collar and lapel lines and appears droopy under the armhole, where the sleeve fits into the garment. This problem can usually be corrected with additional shoulder padding.

Ready-to-wear assumes that a man's shoulders are slightly wider than his hips, but many cutters feel that broad shoulders are accompanied by a full abdomen. Manufacturers aiming at a younger clientele take into account the broad-shouldered, slim-hipped, athletic figure. If you have retained a trim physique, regardless of your age, you might have more success shopping where young men buy their clothes.

Fit of ready-to-wear garments has vastly improved in the past five years, no doubt stimulated by economic pressure. As men have become more fashion conscious and at the same time more independent, they look for clothes that will reflect their new image, and also provide good fit. They will patronize only manufacturers who provide such garb. Cutters have become aware of the fitting problems men face and are striving to meet their needs. We believe that unless your fitting problems are very extreme, you can find a cutter who has your body in mind when he makes his clothes. It is imperative that you know for whom, what age bracket and what physique the manufacturer is styling his garments. You should seek a store or line that caters to your body type, your age, your lifestyle and your personality.

SELF-APPRAISAL

To know what your fitting considerations might be, you must get a clear idea of what your body looks like. It's time to take stock of yourself.

Stand in front of a full-length mirror clothed only in your undershorts. Be objective and honest. Your aim is to make a visual evaluation of your body proportion and balance as determined by your bone structure, the distribution of your flesh, your muscle structure and your adipose or fatty tissue. Use a hand-held mirror to observe your posture and body structure from the side and rear.

To develop good posture, practice standing and moving correctly. Raise the diaphragm, keeping the wrinkles out of your midriff. Lifting the diaphragm will put your shoulders in proper position, because without your even thinking about them, your shoulders will fall into alignment, back and down. Raising your diaphragm will also help to flatten your stomach. Keep your knees slightly flexed, not locked, when standing. Flexed knees create a more relaxed, less tiring stance when you stand and allow your pants to hang from the buttocks without hitting your calves in back. When you walk, keep your eyes directed at eye level. If the eyes fall, everything goes! Walk by swinging your legs from the hips, not the knees, and you will appear to be more energetic.

It is very difficult to be objective about yourself. We know that you are gorgeous, but you have got to be able to recognize any tiny flaws before you can go about improving them. So evaluate the body you see in the mirror. On the pages that follow, you may want to check off your findings so you can refer to them at your convenience.

Body Type

The term "body type" is used to describe the size of the skeletal structure. No particular criteria exist for determining an ideal. The bone structure should balance with the body as a whole, primarily in respect to overall height, width and fatty tissue. It used to be common practice to determine body type by a person's wrist circumference alone, but that evaluation is insufficient. You also need to consider the width of the shoulder, the fullness of the rib cage, and the thickness of the shoulder from front to back.

Body Types Are:

☐ Slim

☐ Medium

☐ Sturdy

ANALYSIS OF PHYSIQUE AND POSTURE

Height

Your apparent height has to do not only with how many inches tall you stand but also with the relationship between your height and your width. A slim man appears taller than a sturdy man of the same actual height. Generally, 6 feet and over is considered tall, 5-foot-8 to 5-foot-11 is considered average, and a man 5-foot-7 and under is considered short.

Men Are:
☐ Tall

☐ Average

☐ Short

Face Shape

To determine your face shape, brush your hair back, close one eye and trace your face as reflected in the bathroom mirror with a silver of soap. Another method is to hold a long pencil near the outer corner of one eye, keeping the pencil perpendicular. Observe the outline of the face which extends beyond the pencil, particularly the location of the width. Your face may be round, oval, square or long.

The ideal face shape is an oval. An oval face is most symmetrical and can wear any hair style the texture of hair will allow. We strive to create the illusion of an oval by hair styling. With maturity, an oval face can appear square because the flesh relaxes along the jawline.

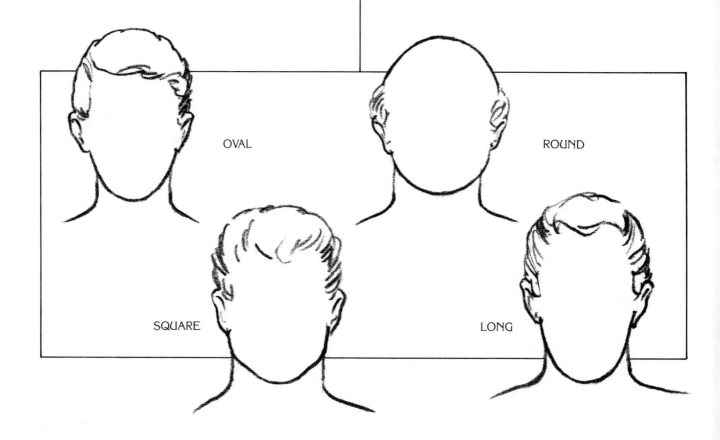

OVAL

ROUND

SQUARE

LONG

Posture And Head Position

View your body from the side, and imagine that a string has been dropped through the middle of your head. If your body is well aligned and your posture good, the string should fall just behind the lobe of your ear, bisect your shoulder and mark the middle of your body. If your posture and head position aren't right, work on them as you think of that string and line them up properly.

Posture Is:
☐ Good

☐ Poor

Head Position Is:
☐ Aligned

☐ Forward

Head Size

Traditionally, the ideal male figure has been considered to be eight heads tall, and male fashion models come close to this measure. This means that the total length of the head, not including hair, would divide into the total body height eight times. The 6-foot-tall, model-type figure often conforms to this proportion. Because of this visual standard, a man with a small head appears to be taller and thinner than one with a large head. The men in fashion ads may stand as tall as twelve heads high. Male clients of the Fashion Academy average about seven and one-half heads tall, which is a a good proportion.

The importance of the head size proportion concerns your hair styling, and it will help to determine whether the hair should be styled in a fuller or more compact style. Your hair affects the apparent size of your head, that is, how large or small it may appear. Small or prominent facial features will also influence how large your head appears. Evaluate your head size according to your visual observations and your feelings about yourself.

Heads May Be:
☐ Small

☐ Proportioned

☐ Large

Upper And Lower Back

The ideal upper back is slightly rounded, reflecting a well-formed spinal column. Your posture, bone structure and fatty tissue can contribute to an overly rounded upper back. Thinness or an angular bone structure can make your upper back appear flat. Ready-to-wear clothing assumes every man has that ideal slightly rounded upper back.

ANALYSIS OF PHYSIQUE AND POSTURE

The term "lower back" refers to the back of the midriff, waist and buttocks. Sometimes we may describe a man as "swaybacked," which means that he has a concave area above round buttocks. Other men, particularly if they have flat rear ends, will be quite flat in the lower back. A flat rear is hard to fit—as is one which is too rounded. A moderate curve is ideal.

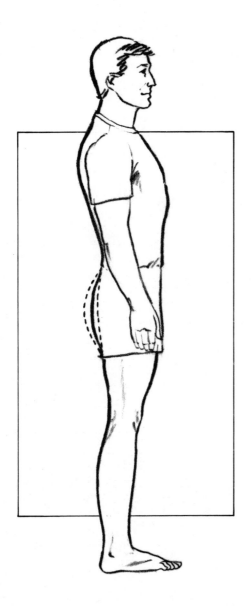

Upper Backs Are:
- ☐ Flat
- ☐ Slightly Rounded
- ☐ Rounded

Lower Backs Are:
- ☐ Flat
- ☐ Slightly Rounded
- ☐ Rounded
- ☐ Swaybacked

Neck Length And Girth

The ideal neck length is a visual perception having to do not only with the neck's actual length but with its sturdiness and slimness as well. The position of your head and the set of your shoulders may affect apparent neck lengths. A forward-set head has a shortening effect on your neck; square shoulders will make your neck appear shorter. The width and length of your neck must be considered when you choose hair styles, collars, and necklines on T-shirts and sweaters.

Neck Length Is:
- ☐ Balanced
- ☐ Short
- ☐ Long

Neck Girth Is:
- ☐ Proportioned
- ☐ Sturdy
- ☐ Slim

Shoulder Width

A well developed, healthy, trim man has shoulders which are wider than his hips. An individual with broad shoulders can gain pounds without the additional weight being particularly noticeable, while someone with narrow shoulders will show every extra pound.

A man who has broad shoulders and slim hips appears to be taller than he is because he is carrying the width of his body higher. The closer your width is to the ground—as with broad hips or a full abdomen—the shorter you look.

Shoulder Width:
☐ Balanced
☐ Broad
☐ Narrow

Shoulder Slope

As we noted earlier in this chapter, all ready-to-wear garments assume that there is a two-inch drop from the base of the neck to the tip of the shoulder. However, we find that most men's shoulders do not drop that much. They are more square. If your shoulders conform approximately to a two-inch drop, we call them tapered. More than a two-inch drop, we call sloped. If your shoulders are more square, estimate the degree of squareness—slightly or very square. If your shoulders vary sufficiently from the hypothetical "norm"—either in being too square or too sloped—you will have a fitting problem.

Shoulder Slope:
☐ Tapered
☐ Sloped
☐ Slightly Square
☐ Very Square

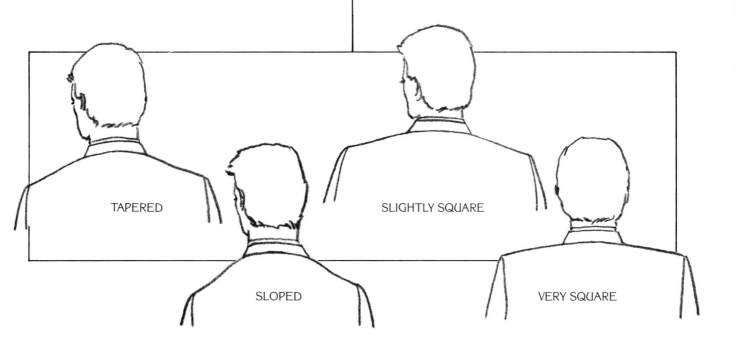

TAPERED

SLOPED

SLIGHTLY SQUARE

VERY SQUARE

ANALYSIS OF PHYSIQUE AND POSTURE

Chest Size

A large rib cage, a pigeon chest or over-developed pectoral muscles present definite fitting problems for men seeking ready-to-wear suits, jackets and shirts. A muscular chest can be very attractive in knitted shirts —or perfectly bare, for that matter. However, few suits provide the necessary room for a heavily-muscled chest, causing gaping lapels on coats and uncomfortable binding across the chest in shirts.

Chest Size:
☐ Narrow
☐ Proportioned
☐ Large

Midriff

The midriff area lies between the chest and the waistline. The more slender your midriff is, the longer it will appear. Your rib cage determines the size of your midriff and whether it looks wide from side to side or from front to back. A slender midriff gives you a younger look and is an absolute necessity if you want to wear slim-cut, high-style clothing.

Midriffs Are:
☐ Slim
☐ Full

Waistline And Stomach

To determine the location of your waist-line, fasten an inch-wide belt snugly around your waist. The bottom of the belt will mark your correct waistline.

The figure problem faced by more men than any other is a too-ample stomach—a paunch or potbelly, to be brutally honest. A spare tire of fatty tissue around the waist-line can make the youngest man appear middle-aged. It is worth any amount of diet or exercise to control this area of your body. If a full waistline is your lot in life, however, you may have to accept that it is there to stay and learn how to live with it, adapting your wardrobe accordingly.

Waistline:
☐ Slim
☐ Medium
☐ Thick

Hips And Thighs

Most men have hips which are flat on the sides. Some men are built with flat hips and a flat rump as well, and we describe them as having "snake hips." With the addition of excess fatty tissue, however, some men develop round hips. Football players and other athletes often develop large thighs because they use their legs with such power. When large thighs are combined with slim hips, there is a fitting problem.

Hips Are:
☐ Flat
☐ Round

Thighs Are:
☐ Slim
☐ Large

Legs

The apparent length of your legs is a visual perception having to do with your total body proportion. Many men who are short automatically assume that they have short legs; tall people decide that theirs are long. These assumptions are not necessarily true. Experience in measuring hundreds of men has proven that the key to their overall height, short or tall, is in their hip and midriff area rather than the legs themselves. If you were to measure your legs from where the body bends when you lift your knee, that is, from where the leg is connected to your hip socket, you will find that your legs are longer than your upper body.

The most important consideration is that *your* leg balances with *your body.*

Leg Lengths Are:
☐ Balanced
☐ Long
☐ Short

Arms

If your figure is in good balance, your elbows will fit neatly into your waistline and the middle knuckle of your thumbs will be even with your crotch when your arms hang loosely at your sides.

Well-proportioned arms are used in determining the proper length for suitcoats. If your arms vary from the ideal—either longer or shorter—you will use your crotch as a guide for coat length. Proper coat lengths are discussed in Chapter III.

Length Of Arms Are:
☐ Short
☐ Balanced
☐ Long

Nobody is perfect. And who should know that better than you, as you try to achieve perfection in your clothing selections? The trick is to discover and accept your body's occasional variations from the physical ideal and learn to camouflage or hide them. That is the secret: Hide your bad points and play up the good ones with careful choices of clothing.

Suiting Yourself

3

FITTING THE STYLE TO YOU

Now that you have come to grips with the shape you're in, let's examine the options you have in selecting clothing which will emphasize the positive and camouflage the negative.

The look that most men like is determined by what the well-dressed and affluent are wearing. In the United States, men buy ready-to-wear suits that reflect the tastes of those trend-setters.

MIDRIFF

SKIRT

Mass-produced clothing in America has graduated from the early influence of the Brooks Brothers sack, designed with the mature or portly figure in mind, to other styles. American designers adopted the extremely shaped or fitted suit from Europe and London's Saville Row for a while. The stiff rope shoulder and extremely high armhole suggested by Italian menswear looked dashing on the few men whose bodies could tolerate the restrictiveness. American men, however, are devoted to comfort. They are now into body building, and our dominant national image is one of rugged individualism. The American male wants to look fashionable—as long as he can still move, sit, drive his car and enjoy a business lunch comfortably in what he's wearing.

The designer influence, tempered with this demand for comfort, has evolved into what we might call "American Styling." The "American Style" suit is actually what well-dressed men have worn for years—those who could afford custom tailoring, that is. The cut is flexible enough so that it reflects the man as an individual. Instead of the suit wearing the man, its construction is soft enough to mold to his body. The "American Style" suit has gentle shaping in the midriff, ease in the skirt, a moderately high armhole (which incidentally affords more movement than a low armhole) and padded shoulders. Thus, the appeal of this cut is that it allows for variation depending on each man's physique and personality.

EUROPEAN
STYLE

Men have less opportunity for conceal-ment than women do with their clothes because the basic menswear style offerings are limited. However, within the selection of pants, coats and shirts are more options than you might have imagined.

In order to introduce you to your options and explain men's clothing in its simplest form, we use the term "silhouette." Silhou-ette describes the basic cut or shape of a garment exclusive of any decoration. The silhouette should be your primary considera-tion when you go to purchase any suit, jacket or pant; it must be correct for your body, your personality and your lifestyle.

We call the basic silhouette "STRUC-TURAL DESIGN." Anything added to it in the form of pockets, lapels, buttons, yokes, plackets, vents, shoulder treatments, trim and the like is "APPLIED DESIGN." Applied design is used to add interest and function to a garment. It can "reconstruct the architec-ture" or improve the visual balance of the body. Applied design, along with fabric texture and pattern, is the most effective way you can express your personality.

We have divided jackets into five basic silhouettes which will be determined by your body proportion—your posture, the balance of your shoulders to your hips, the condition of your abdomen and midriff, your height and your fatty tissue.

The trick is to have your suit fit snugly, as if it were molded to your body, and still allow you to move comfortably. If the suit has enough room so that you can nearly touch your elbows together in front, however, it will be sloppy across the back. A suit is intended to make a strong visual impact when you enter, leave, stand, walk and sit. It is not designed for playing ball or even for driving long distances.

FITTING THE STYLE TO YOU

FIVE BASIC JACKET SILHOUETTES

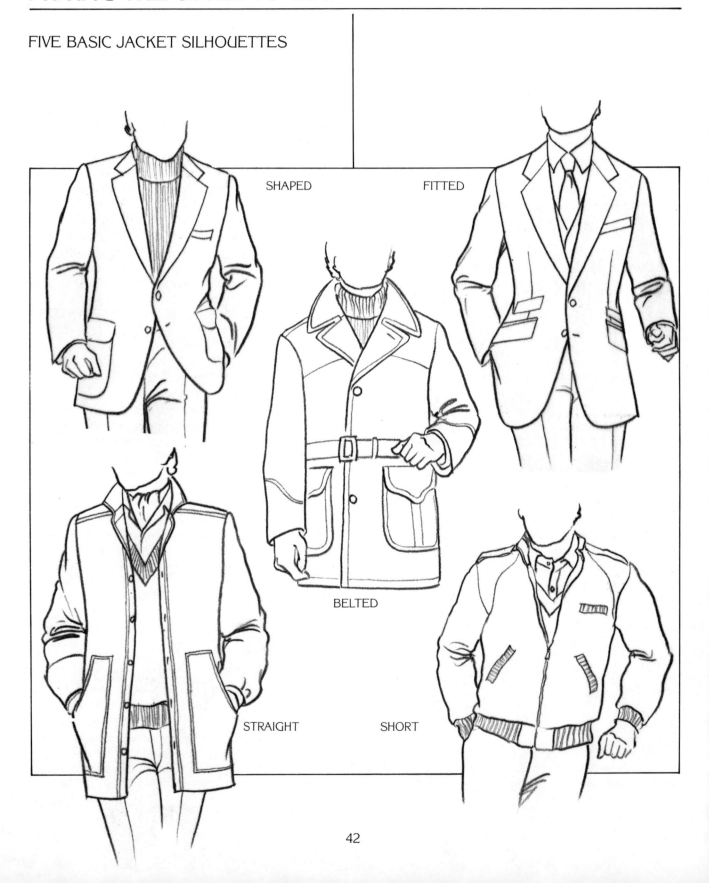

SHAPED

FITTED

BELTED

STRAIGHT

SHORT

Shaped Jacket

We generally think of a sport coat when we provide an example of the shaped jacket silhouette. The shaped jacket has moderate shaping in the side seams and occasionally a few darts or seams incorporated in the pocket treatment or over double vents in the back.

All men can wear the shaped jacket. Even a portly or heavy man will benefit from the shaping it provides in the area just below the armpit or midriff section and in the back. The jacket's lower-back contour looks very attractive on most men. Its shaping in the midriff is more flattering than shaping at the actual waistline because it lengthens the leg and therefore gives a more fashionable and slimmer look.

The suit of a sturdy or heavy man will have a shaped jacket rather than one that is fitted. The heavy man's coat should never be really snug, but the shaping creates an illusion of relative slimness.

The taller, slimmer man who might utilize more fitted styling in his suits will wear shaped sports jackets because they offer a more casual, comfortable look. The sleeve of a sport coat will be more ample, the shoulders a bit wider, the armhole lower than in more fitted styles. The sport jacket should allow enough room to be worn as an outdoor coat over sport shirts or sweaters.

Sport coats are usually made of softer or more textured fabrics such as flannel, fleece, Ultra Suede and the like. Suits, on the other hand, are usually made of hard-finish menswear worsted fabrics. We do see some casual suits of flannel with patch pockets and other styling with which an alternate pair of slacks may be worn, but the jacket of the average dress suit can never double as a sport coat. Most suit coats will go with their own slacks and nothing else.

Fitted Jacket Or Suit Coat

The American Style suit is a modification by American designers of the more extreme European styling. A most becoming, wearable silhouette, its shape follows the general lines of the body. It has moderately broad and lightly padded shoulders, a gently nipped-in waist, a comfortable skirt and a moderately high armhole. "Blades," or soft folds of extra fabric in front and in back near the armhole, allow arm and shoulder movement.

The fitted silhouette has been the choice of fine dressers for decades. The fitted jacket symbolizes youth, success and affluence; it epitomizes the "power look." You need a slim midriff and waistline to wear the fitted jacket, but it is worth all the dieting and workouts you may have to do to maintain your physique so that this silhouette looks good on you.

The fit of this flattering coat is in the midriff area, rather than at the waistline itself. Raising the emphasis of fit gives your body a slimmer look and visually lengthens your legs for a longer, more fashionable appearance. The amount of nipping at the sides, in front and in back can vary according to your personality and individual taste.

The shoulder styling may present a more continental look, which is fairly square and has more padding, or a natural shoulder, which in American suits indicates moderate padding. Whichever styling you may choose, be aware that all shoulders benefit from padding. It is not necessarily intended to make the shoulders look more square, but it gives a smooth and elegantly tailored look to the garment. A man who would like to appear a little taller or slimmer will benefit from slightly more padding. Broad shoulders make the body appear slimmer.

Shaping comes from seams. This explains why double vents are so becoming: The extra seams in back provide more opportunity for shaping. The man with a slim waist and midriff benefits from the additional fitting afforded by double seams. Meanwhile, the thicker man benefits from the slimming effect of the seaming itself, which creates an

FITTING THE STYLE TO YOU

illusion of thinness underneath. The length of the vent opening is important. It should be no more than 8 inches long, and shorter on a shorter man.

CAUTION: If you have a full abdomen or a roll of flab around your waist, you cannot wear the fitted silhouette. You can achieve some shaping with your jacket's side seams, but the garment must barely skim the body rather than fit snugly. Any clothing which is too tight will emphasize fatty tissue.

Straight Coat Or Jacket

The straight or box jacket is not often seen in suits or sport coats, except in portly sizes. This silhouette is primarily found in leisure jackets or shirts, lumberjack shirts, and quilted or cold-weather coats. The straight jacket was part of the "leisure suit" ensemble during the early '70s—a style which, fortunately, enjoyed very brief popularity. Leisure suits were made of polyester double knits, often in light colors, and the only men who looked less than atrocious in them were small Gamin men. (The term Gamin will be explained in a later chapter on personality.) The straight jacket has not yet recovered from the negative impact of the leisure suit, but it is still the most popular silhouette in outdoor gear.

The straight jacket silhouette looks good on the man with broad shoulders, a full chest and narrow hips. It provides great camouflage for a full abdomen or a thick waist, because a man needs some substance in those areas to fill the jacket out. Skinny men do not wear this silhouette well.

The straight jacket looks best if its length reaches to the crotch, thus retaining all possible leg length to provide a sense of tallness. Tall men can wear the straight jacket longer.

If you own a hunter's shirt or lightweight jacket with a straight silhouette, you might consider having it shaped in the side seams if the shaped jacket provides a more flattering look for you.

Belted Jacket

The belted jacket silhouette is great for casual wear, but never buy a belted dress suit because a belt will date a suit.

A belt on the back of a jacket will emphasize a slim middle. If the skirt of the belted jacket is ample, it will camouflage thick hips. However, only a slim, well-proportioned body can wear a belted jacket attractively. For instance, thin men and tall men look marvelous in the safari jacket and the Marine Corps belted dress uniform. As with any style which can be worn well only by a limited number of people, the belted jacket is not an often-featured fashion item.

Short Jacket

There are as many designs and cuts and fabrics found in the short jacket as there are people to wear them. You can spend from five dollars to five hundred, depending on whether you want inexpensive nylon or buttery leather. Traditionally known as the windbreaker, Eisenhower, bomber's, Members Only, jogging or Levi jacket, it is a perennial favorite for casual wear.

This is the most versatile silhouette for sports or casual wear. It can be found in all lengths, stopping at the waistline, dropping to the hip or falling anywhere in between. The short jacket is becoming on all body types because it exposes the maximum amount of leg and broadens the shoulder. The shorter the jacket, the slimmer the hips should be which show under it. The man with small hips can emphasize them with a shorter jacket, while the fuller-hipped man will look better with a longer version of the windbreaker.

The most important point to remember if you are exposing your derriere by wearing a short jacket or windbreaker is that your pants must fit properly!

FITTING THE STYLE TO YOU

APPLIED DESIGN IN JACKETS

Jackets offer four different arrangements of buttons. The most becoming and easiest to wear is the two-button style. A one-button is not for the full-chested man, because the single low button leaves a long lapel which tends to gap open over a full chest. The one-button style is seen in dinner jackets and has been used in casual sport jackets.

The three-button style is an Ivy League look, with the middle button being the one which is buttoned. However, this can look sloppy. The poorly reinforced lapel—once

TWO-BUTTON

ONE-BUTTON

FITTING THE STYLE TO YOU

tailored with hair canvas interfacing, now mass-produced with iron-on interfacing for ready-to-wear garments—often rolls down to the secured middle button, leaving the top buttonhole glaring from the displaced roll line.

The two-button or four-button double-breasted suit needs to be worn buttoned. The Classic man is willing to take the trouble to button his jacket every time he stands up and to unbutton it when he sits. Other men will not be bothered, however.

THREE-BUTTON

DOUBLE-BREASTED

Buttons

Buttons should look expensive and match the color of the suit. Metal buttons provide a more sporty feeling and may be found on sport suits or blazer jackets.

There should be buttons on the sleeves of jackets, but working buttonholes are rarely found on sleeves today, even on expensive suits. The only working buttonhole you'll need, other than those on the front of your jacket, is on the lapel, especially if you have ever considered sporting a flower there.

You can upgrade the quality of many jackets by upgrading the quality of their buttons.

Lapels

The lapels of a well-styled suit should extend to just a fraction less than the halfway mark between your collar and your shoulderline. The lapels should be in balance with the other parts of the jacket.

NOTCHED

SEMI-PEAKED

FITTING THE STYLE TO YOU

Several types of lapels are found on jackets:

Notched — The notched lapel is the most classic and has the most staying power fashionwise.

Semi-peaked — this collar comes and goes in fashion. It is often an expression of high styling in a suit. If the peak is moderate, it will not necessarily date your suit.

Peaked — This is an extreme style which is more often found on the double-breasted suit. A suit with peaked lapels is not a good investment unless you can afford to leave it in the back of your closet, waiting for the fashion cycle to come around again in about five to ten years.

Shawl — This style is most usually seen on tuxedos. It also was used in the casual, unconstructed jackets that young men wore in the '70s. Though not a basic look, it could add variety to the wardrobe of a young-at-heart, tall, slim man.

PEAKED

SHAWL

Yokes And Epaulets

Yokes are a flattering detail found on Western dress suits or sport coats, but they make a poor investment on a traditional dress suit. Use yokes on casual Western shirts and jackets. The shaped Western yoke with back seam is guaranteed to make all shoulders look broader and waists slimmer.

FITTING THE STYLE TO YOU

Epaulets are found on sport jackets such as windbreakers and on summer cotton shirts. A detail adapted from the military, epaulets look good on everyone except those men with very broad or square shoulders. In addition, men with short necks do not benefit from epaulets.

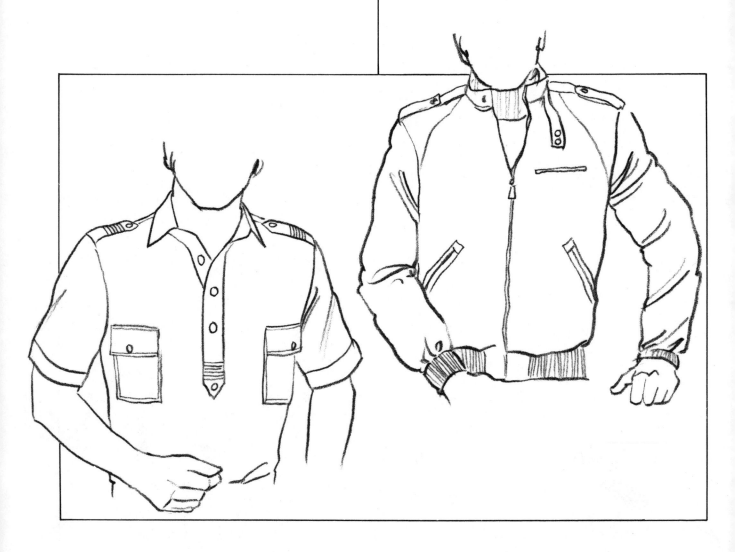

Vents

The center vent is most commonly found on jackets, probably because it is cheapest to produce. However, it gives no help in shaping the silhouette in spite of looking good. The double vent provides a better opportunity for shaping and looks good on all men except those with large, rounded buttocks. As we

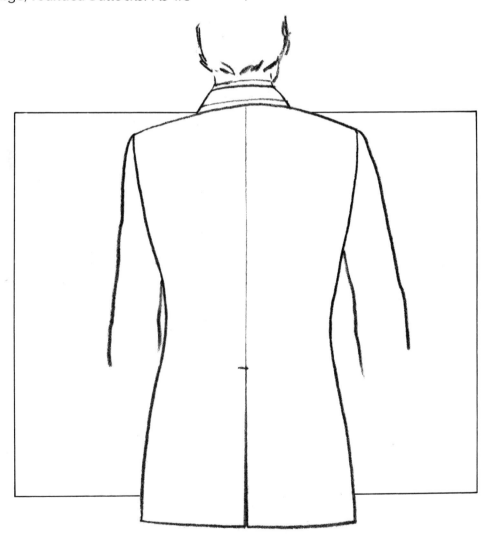

FITTING THE STYLE TO YOU

noted earlier, no vent should be cut higher than 8 inches.

Side vents are casual and attractive, especially for those men who love to put their hands in their pants pockets. Just remember, vents are a styling element, not an aspect of fit. Never depend on their expansion to get your coat to go around your hips.

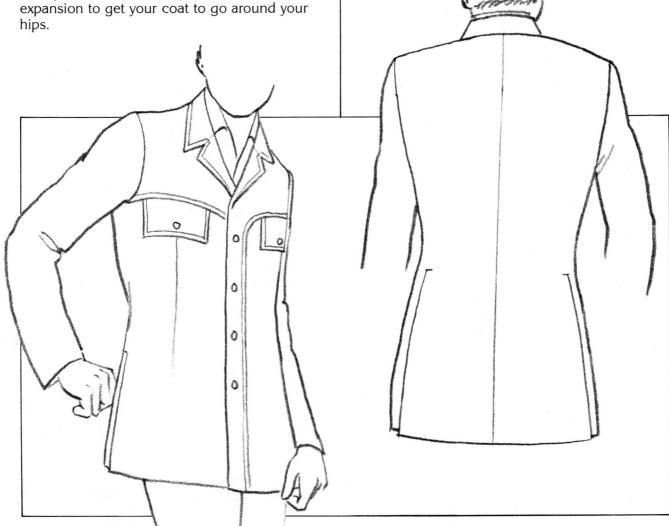

Pocket Types On Jackets

Pockets fall into two basic types, the patch and the inset. An inset pocket may or may not have a flap; the preferred type has a flap which may be tucked in. The patch pocket, found on casual suits and sport coats, can be plain or very ornate.

For detail on a patch pocket to look good, you need to be tall and slender. A plain patch pocket with matching top stitching looks good on all figure types.

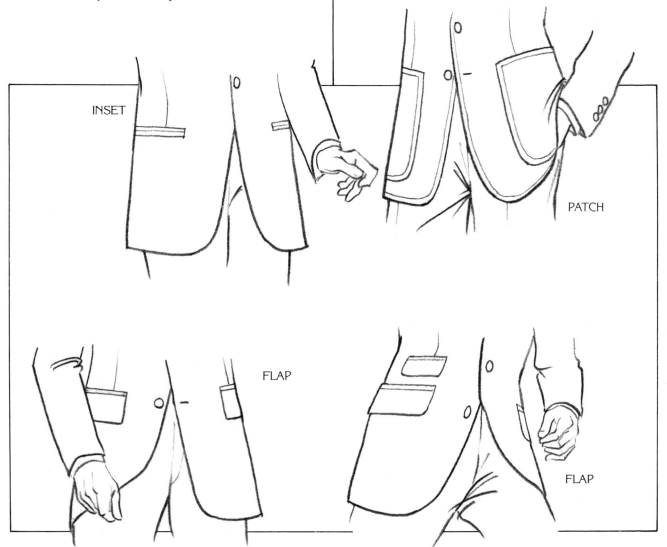

INSET

PATCH

FLAP

FLAP

FITTING THE STYLE TO YOU

Jacket Bottom Finish

The most flattering hem on the bottom of a jacket is curved in front. It appears to lengthen the leg. A straight hem is found on the double-breasted suit and often on the one-button jacket as well. The straight-bottomed jacket should be worn a little shorter than one with a curved bottom.

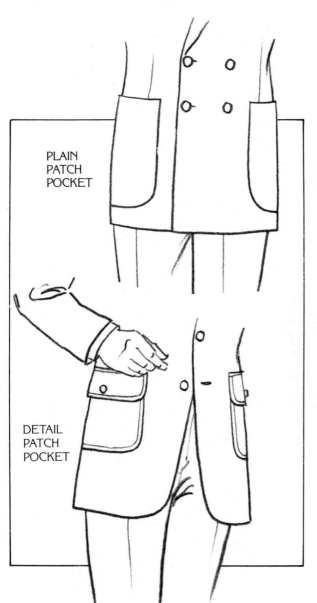

PLAIN
PATCH
POCKET

DETAIL
PATCH
POCKET

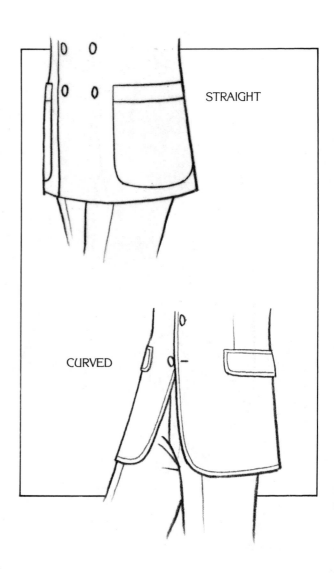

STRAIGHT

CURVED

VESTS

Vests should fit like a second skin, covering the waistband of your trousers and just barely showing above your suit lapels when the suit is buttoned. The bottom button of the vest is always left undone. Your trousers must always come up to your waistline so that your shirt or belt does not show under the vest.

RIGHT

WRONG

FITTING THE STYLE TO YOU

To add variety to your wardrobe, you might want to add a lightweight flannel, velveteen or doeskin vest in white, a bright color or a pattern. A light vest can give a dark suit an added touch of elegance. Bright or patterned vests look best with casual wear. The vest could also be a sleeveless V-neck sweater for wear with a sport coat.

TIPS ON FITTING A SUIT

A look of naturalness and ease is what makes a suit right for a man. A dress suit should be fairly snug; a wrinkle here and there can still fall within the definition of good fit. In fact, a few wrinkles suggest the comfortable nonchalance so typical of the American male. The success of your suit is determined when you purchase it, so careful selection and attention to detail are essential.

Suit sizing varies with different cutters. Try a larger and smaller size in the same brand. Depending on your height, try the short, regular and long, regardless of what you have been accustomed to buying. The proportions of the whole suit—including position of the armhole, location of the buttons and the shaping—are affected by its length. These proportions will vary with different cutters, sometimes even with the same cutter, according to the designated length of the suit.

Dress well when you go shopping for a suit. Wear a dress shirt, a tie and good shoes. Dressing well not only gains you the respect of salespeople, but it also gives you a sound foundation of shoes and shirt to enhance any garment you might try on.

Determine which suits you might try by following this game plan: Find the area in the store where your size or range of sizes is presented. Decide if there is a color among the group which will work for you. Then try on the jacket to determine whether the suit has the right silhouette, fabric and applied design for you. Most tailors prefer to fit the pants before they make adjustments to other pieces of the suit. If adjustments are minor, the tailor can then fit the jacket over the pants. However, if the pants need major adjustments or you can't keep your perspective because of the unhemmed pants, have the jacket fitted over your own pants.
See pages 18 and 19

Evaluate the fit of the jacket:

1. The collar should curve smoothly around the back of your neck. About one-half inch of shirt collar should show above the suit collar in back.

2. The jacket should ride flat on your shoulders without buckling or creasing.

3. The fabric should follow the curve of your upper back and snug into the contour of your lower back. Try on many brands and observe very carefully how each suit fits your back. This can be a tricky area to fit, because very little shaping can be accomplished in a center back seam.

4. The lapels should hug your chest, and there should be a happy marriage of shirt collar and suit lapel.

5. The width of the jacket shoulders is critical. Most men buy their suits too large. For a proper fit, the fabric of the upper sleeve should just barely skim the flesh of the upper arm in a suit. The fit of a sports jacket can be looser, but a good dress suit is snug.

6. Most men will find a wrinkle of excess fabric below the collar in back. This is caused by having shoulders more square than the suit or by an erect posture. This wrinkle can be removed by pushing the excess fabric up into the collar seam. If this is an alteration you require, make certain that you try on the suit *after* the tailor has done his work, so you can ascertain that too much fabric has not been removed. Too much will cause the coat to pull outward from the body at the waist and make the suit appear shorter in back than in front. A jacket which has been overaltered and hangs away from the body in back is destroyed.

7. Place the paraphernalia you normally carry into the pockets to check for fit. Few suits can accommodate the volume of stuff that most men take with them. If this proves to be a problem for you, buy a wrist or shoulder bag or a briefcase.

8. Ideally, the threads of the sleeve at the upper arm will run relatively horizontal to the floor. As we noted in the previous chapter, your arm should hang in the middle of the sleeve with approximately the same amount of room in front and in back of it. If your arm hits the back of the sleeve, there will be diagonal wrinkles running from the cap of the sleeve in front toward the elbow in back.

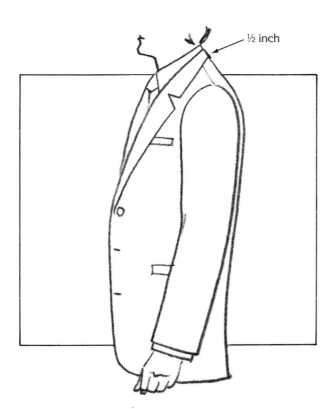

½ inch

Tailors of ready-to-wear do not tackle sleeves. If the sleeves of a jacket you're considering do not hang properly on your frame, look for another suit. Incidentally, this condition seems to bear no relationship to the quality of the suit. It has solely to do with how the sleeve is inserted into the armhole. Sleeve hang could be improved on most suits if cutters would rotate the sleeve slightly toward the front.

9. Raise your arms, relax, twist your body and bend to test the fit of the coat. Temporary posture improvement reveals nothing. Stand naturally.

10. Armholes should be set comfortably high on a suit coat; on a sport coat, they can be lower. A high armhole allows more fredom of movement than a low armhole. Those in sport coats are set lower to allow for sweaters to be worn underneath.

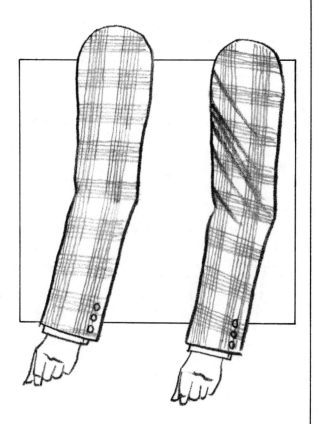

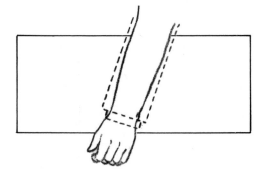

11. Suit sleeves should be hemmed so that they barely cover the wristbones when the arms hang relaxed. One-half inch of shirt cuff will show. Sport coats can be a fraction longer, particularly if you prefer short-sleeved sport shirts.

12. The skirt of a suit should be of ample cut. Vents must be basted closed for fitting so you won't depend on their spreading open to achieve enough girth. The waist will appear slimmer if the skirt fits loosely. Even a slender man will look more fashionable with the slimness accentuated in his midriff and waist by leaving some flare in the skirt of the suit.

13. The length of the jacket should be as short as it can be while still conforming to current fashion. It should adequately cover the curve of your buttocks. The best way to judge good jacket length is to be sure the jacket reaches about one inch below your crotch (not the pant crotch unless the pants are perfectly fitted). This is more effective than the old "rule of thumb," which assumed all men's arms and thumbs were the same length.

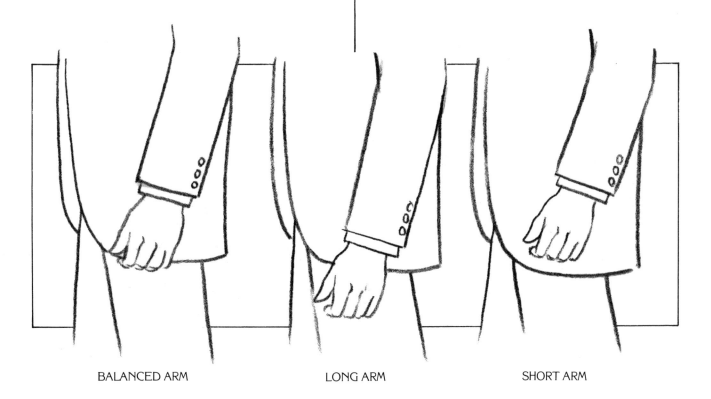

BALANCED ARM   LONG ARM   SHORT ARM

FITTING THE STYLE TO YOU

PANTS

There are three basic silhouettes in the cut of pants: The straight, the flared and the tapered. Trouser tops come in two styles: Pleated or plain front.

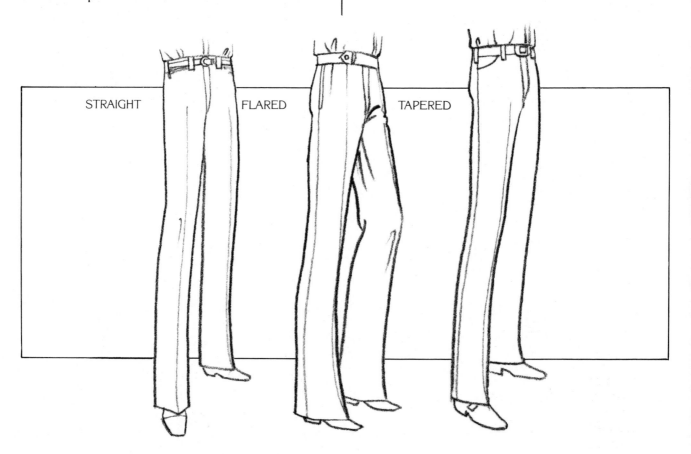

STRAIGHT   FLARED   TAPERED

Straight Pants

The straight pant is the one which stays in style because it is by far the most becoming on all figure types. It will accomplish even more in terms of attractiveness if it is slightly shaped just above the knee. The width of the pant at the bottom should be related to the size of your foot—a skimpy cut will emphasize a large foot. Of even greater importance than foot size is the spot on the foot where the pants hit. A skimpy pant leg will hit the instep of the shoe, requiring the pant to be at least one inch shorter than a pant leg of more generous cut. Ideally, the pant will barely skim the foot at the toe of the shoe and drop slightly toward the back, giving maximum length to the leg. A slight break, or a wrinkle above where the pant hits the shoe, is favored by some clothiers. Some feel that the slight break brings the eye to the hemline of the pant and lengthens the leg. It is a matter of taste. Just make certain that if you do have a break, it is a slight one.

Flared Pants

The flared pant is very becoming provided the flare is slight. The indentation or shaping of the leg should be above the knee, where it creates a young look and has a lengthening effect on the leg. Above-the-knee shaping also allows the flare to begin above the calf, an arrangement helpful for the man with a hyper-extended calf. Pants with no more than a one-inch difference between the above-knee measure and hem are conservative enough to remain in style.

A more extreme flare in pants is a fashion innovation reminiscent of the bell-bottomed trousers of the U.S. Navy, which require the wearer to have small hips and well proportioned thighs to look good. It is a fact that the wider hemline on bell-bottomed pants accentuated the slim hips of sailors and contributed to their young, flamboyant, sexy appearance.

Pants with extreme flare had their day in the '70s and will not reappear on the fashion scene for many years.

Tapered Pants

The idea of pants following the natural contour of the body, tapering slowly from waist to ankle, sounds good but just doesn't work in practice. The visual impact of tapered pants with skimpy cuffs is to make the hips appear larger. This fact, coupled with the way the hem of the pant hits the foot, a full inch shorter than straight or flared pants, eliminates this look except for very tall, thin men.

The effect is more pleasing if the pant tapers to just above the knee and then falls, with the fabric at the inseam and outseam cut perfectly straight with the grain of the threads.

The popularity of one common tapered pant style—jeans—is epidemic worldwide. They can be the backbone of a leisure-time wardrobe. Jeans definitely follow the contour of the body. The only thing is, a man should be sure that he wants his contour followed. Why any man over 50 or overweight would want to wear jeans when he would look infinitely better in a good pair of slacks, escapes us. Like so much in fashion, jeans are for the very young or the slim.

FITTING THE STYLE TO YOU

APPLIED DESIGN ON PANTS
Trouser Tops

Basically, there are two styles of trouser tops: Pleated or plain front. Plain front pants give a trimmer look but are somewhat restricting. Trouser pleats offer more room in the crotch and hip area. Some men have trouble adjusting to the pleated look, having been raised in slim-fitting pants, but once they adjust, they enjoy pleats. The keys to attractive-looking trouser pleats are an easy drape in the fabric and good fit. You shouldn't have a whole wardrobe of pleated pants, but they remain an option you should consider.

Suit Pants

For suit pants, the simpler the design the better. If suit pants ride at your waistline or slightly above, your waist will look smaller and your stomach flatter. American men have grown up in Levi's jeans and tend to push all trousers down on the hips, thus passing up a slimming style possibility. Suit pants are cut and hemmed to ride at the waistline, so the fit of the crotch and the length of the pant will be destroyed if you push them down. The best advice for men with a full abdomen or midriff, or those with snake hips for that matter, is to wear braces or suspenders with your suits. Suspenders assure the smooth, comfortable hang of suit pants and are absolutely indispensable for dancing.

Pants Pockets

The three basic pocket styles in trousers are side seam, slanted and Western. Pockets should fit flat without pulling at the sides, which means that there must be ample room in the pants. Custom tailors prefer the Western pocket because it does not gap. Otherwise, the pocket styles you choose are a matter of what you like best.

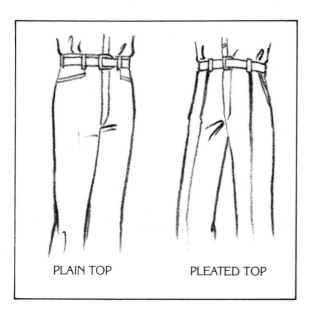

PLAIN TOP   PLEATED TOP

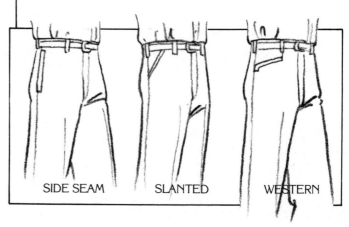

SIDE SEAM   SLANTED   WESTERN

Fads In Pants

As far as the trendier garments are concerned, your choice will usually fall in the sportswear category. Have as many fad garments as your budget or personality will allow. Remember, however, that the more

Pant Cuffs

Cuffs are neither in nor out—they are a matter of taste. The tall Classic man wears cuffs most successfully of any personality type. If you are trying to achieve more length in the leg, don't wear cuffs because cuffs

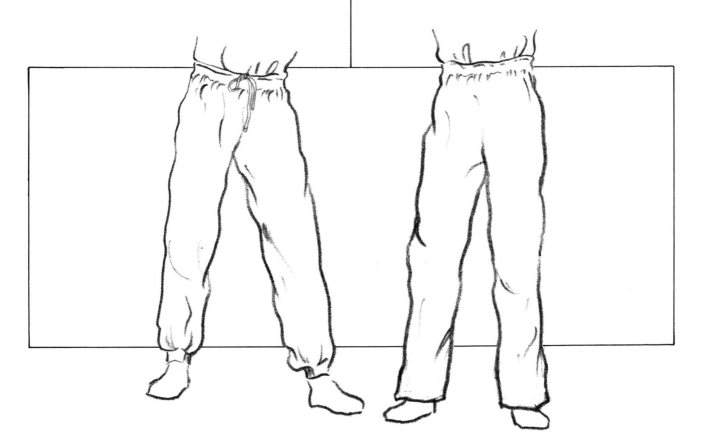

"IN" a garment is this year, the more "OUT" it will be next year. Many of the trendy styles are adapted from genuine active sportswear or the military. If you choose styles which are very close to the original utilitarian design, they will enjoy a longer fashion life.

cannot drop in the back. This is a matter of particular concern to the short or heavy man.

Cuffs on a flare leg flop when a man walks.

FITTING THE STYLE TO YOU

FIT OF PANTS

The biggest problem in fitting pants comes when you buy a suit. If you have big shoulders and slim hips, the pants will inevitably be too large. The length or rise of a crotch cannot be altered, so if the slacks of the suit do not fit reasonably well in the crotch, do not buy the suit. You will have to find a suit by a different cutter.

The traditional place for a tailor to alter the waistline of pants is in the center back seam. Taking in that seam too much requires that the threads or grain of the fabric make a turn from the leg to where it is sewn into the center seam. When fabric direction is changed, wrinkles are created below the buttocks. The grain of the threads ideally should be allowed to run up the back of the leg, across the buttocks to the waistband.

When too much fabric is removed at the center back, either at the time of cutting or during alterations, the fit of the pants under the buttocks is destroyed.

When cutters come to realize that fabric wants to hang straight or "on grain," and they learn to cut pants accordingly, men's pants will fit better.

In the meantime, if your waist is slim you would get a better fit if the altering were done in the side seams rather than the center seam. Not many tailors will tackle that job, and sometimes the pocket location will not allow it. Few tailors understand what is needed. If you find a jewel who does, he or she will charge extra for the work. However, if he or she is skilled, it is worth the extra money.

Take plenty of time to adjust pants to your waistline before having them marked for hemming. Pants which later slide down below a full abdomen destroy the appearance of the whole suit. Wear suspenders!

Have pants hemmed so they barely skim the shoe in front and then drop slightly in the back. This gives a slimmer look.

The fit, fabric and pockets of pants are destroyed by the volume of items the average man carries in his pockets: An inch-thick wallet, 15 keys on one ring, an enormous handkerchief, $20 in change, a pocket knife and a comb. A fat wallet carried in the back pocket can be the root of back pain. The most practical solution is to carry a wrist or shoulder bag or briefcase. If this suggestion does not fit into your lifestyle, you must make some adjustments. Get rid of the wallet. You don't need half of the papers and plastic cards you carry. Get a thin billfold for your essential cards and a money clip for currency. Eliminate the less essential keys; you could hide them in your car. Carry most items in your jacket. The only thing you should carry in your pants pockets is your money. Most men leave their pennies at home.

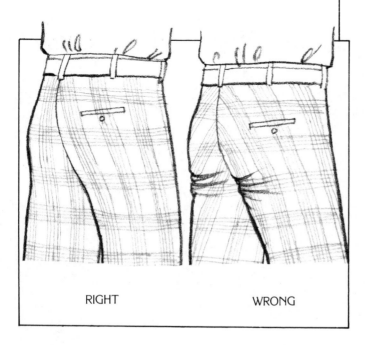

RIGHT   WRONG

DRESS SHIRTS

When worn with a tie under a suit or sport jacket, the collar and one-half inch of cuff are about all anyone sees of a dress shirt. The collar represents the major style contribution of the shirt. Light colors—white, off-white, pastels and ice tones—are always correct for business or dress functions. Never wear a dark-colored shirt with a suit for business or dress. Medium to dark colors are appropriate for sport or casual wear. White shirts are the most formal.

There is a limitless selection of shirt collars, but they can be categorized into five basic types.

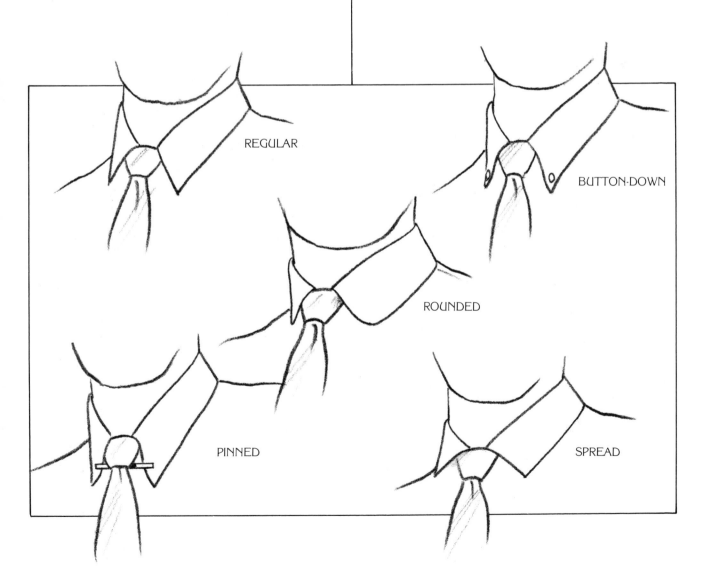

REGULAR

BUTTON-DOWN

ROUNDED

PINNED

SPREAD

FITTING THE STYLE TO YOU

The most important thing to consider is the relationship of the shirt collar to your facial features and your overall physique. A big man with a large face and full neck doesn't want a tiny collar under his chin. Conversely, a high-set collar and 4-inch points will overwhelm a small man with a small face and features.

"Collar points" describe the length of the front edge of the collar from neck edge to point. For the average man wearing a regular collar, the points should be between 2-1/2 and 3-1/4 inches long. The length would depend on the size and personality of the man and the length of his face and neck. Current fashion affects the length of points but, regardless of fashion whims, points of varied lengths are always available.

Regular Collar

The regular collar is the standard one worn by most men. It is simple and correct and can be worn for daytime, evening, sporty or dressy occasions. It suits every shape of face and is appropriate with any suit style. The four-in-hand is the correct tie knot to wear with the regular collar.

Button-Down Collar

The button-down collar with a roll is soft and sporty. This collar is becoming to any face shape. It looks good with sportswear, business suits and all casual wear. The four-in-hand knot goes best with the button-down collar.

Rounded Collar

The rounded collar can be worn with or without a pin. It provides a softer look than the straight-point regular collar and can be worn for sport or dress. A white rounded collar with a colored shirt is a young and handsome look. The four-in-hand knot goes well with the rounded collar.

Pinned Collar

The pinned collar gives your suit a more formal, dressy look. Make sure the collar you pin does not have too wide a spread. The pin itself should be between 1-5/8 and 1-7/8 inches long. The four-in-hand tie knot can be worn with the pinned collar.

Spread Or Cutaway Collar

This style is dressy and dramatic. It looks best on the man with a long, narrow face; it's not for the man with a short, sturdy neck or a round or broad face. The spread or cutaway collar goes well with high-styled suits and can be worn for dress or casual wear. It is appropriate for dinner and the theatre if the shirt fabric is dressy (fine broadcloth). The spread between the points of this collar is spacious enough for a Windsor knot.

FABRIC FOR DRESS SHIRTS

The smoother the fabric, the dressier the shirt. Textured fabric is more casual. The best shirt fabric is fine, long-staple cotton. Fine cotton is as elegant as silk and provides the optimum in comfort. If you can afford the time, expense and bother of a laundry service, by all means buy 100% cotton shirts. But be warned: American women have forgotten how to iron, and men never learned. As a consequence, 100%-cotton shirts present a real challenge. If your shirts will be laundered at home, your best buy is a cotton-polyester blend in a fabric which looks like 100% cotton.

There is no such thing as a genuine wash-and-wear shirt. The collar, cuffs and front band need spray starch and a swipe with an iron. If you snatch your shirts out of the dryer while still warm, there is little need to iron the entire shirt, especially if you wear a jacket. The collar, cuffs and front band, however, will benefit from the shiny, smooth effect achieved by light starch and an iron. The implication is that you are attentive and affluent enough to send your shirts to the laundry.

Most dress shirts are made of broadcloth which has a smooth, fine weave. Oxford cloth has a slight texture and looks a little less dressy. You will want some shirts of each type.

Wash shirts by themselves, never with other dirty or dark-colored laundry. If your shirts have become a trifle dingy from abuse, a professional laundry can sometimes restore them.

CUFFS

The barrel cuff is the basic cuff. It is found with one or two buttons. The two-button barrel cuff is dressier.

A French cuff is twice the length of the barrel. Folded back and held together with cuff links, it provides an elegant look, worth the bother of inserting the links.

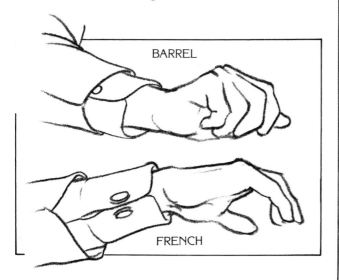

BARREL

FRENCH

FIT OF SHIRTS

Try on shirts until you find the one cut for your torso, and then stay with that brand as much as possible. If your shirt has too much girth in the body, have the side seams shaped or add darts.

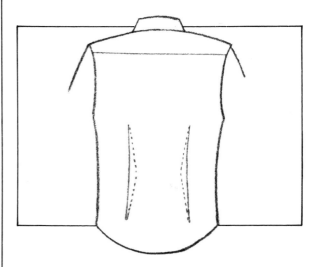

In buying shirts, consider the style and then the size. Shirt size is determined by the circumference of the neck and the length of the arm. To measure for collar size, place a measuring tape around your neck, below your Adam's apple. Swallow to see if it feels comfortable. Then read the measurement to the nearest half-inch, using the higher measure if you fall in between. For sleeves, measure from the prominent vertebra at the base of your neck, over the shoulder and down the arm to the point below your wrist bone where your wrist bends. Have your arm relaxed. Ready-to-wear shirts are often sized with two measures, i.e., 34-35. We have discovered that the sleeve usually matches the lower measure, so buy accordingly. If you have muscular arms or shoulders, you may need extra length. The only foolproof way to buy a shirt is to try it on. It is always better to have your shirt too long than too short because if a shirt sleeve is too long, you can set the buttons over slightly. A snug cuff will allow the shirt sleeve to hit the top of your hand at the proper point, allowing one-half inch of linen to show below the suit jacket.

Do not buy short-sleeved dress shirts. The cuff must show under a dress suit. Short-sleeved shirts are good as sport shirts and as work shirts in hot climates when worn without a jacket. If your dress shirts go to

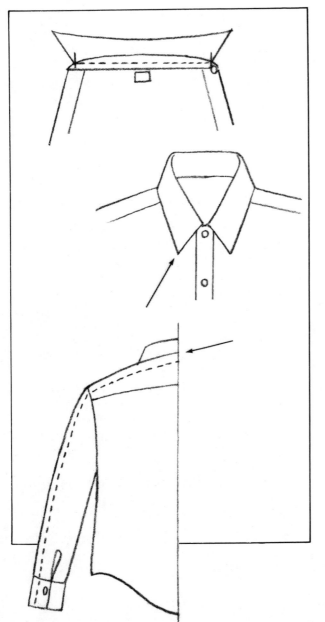

work, buy long sleeves and roll them up for hot weather or hard work.

Shirts should extend about 8 inches below the waist, but not so long that they create bulk in the crotch.

TIES

A tie is the most conspicuous and decorative item in your wardrobe. It outshines the dark tones and muted plaids of your business suits, furnishing a chunk of color close to your face. With men's fashions for business and dress as regimented as they are, your tie is one of the few ways you can express your personality. It is the beacon of your soul.

You should select your tie according to its:

Color — Determined by the color of your suit or your shirt.

Pattern — Influenced by the pattern of your shirt and suit.

Personality — Expressed in the type of fabric, its texture and drape.

The sheen of silky fabric complements a suit or sport coat of dull wool. In addition, silky, lustrous, richly colored ties go with dress suits. By contrast, the rough texture of a knitted tie or textured linen fabric emphasizes a sport coat or textured fabric. Your first decision, then, will be based on the fabric of the jacket with which your tie will be worn. Are you looking for a silky dress tie or a sporty tie?

The color of the tie should be one of the colors of your season; if so, it will harmonize with the suit or jacket you plan to wear. For the most impact, you would do best to coordinate a darker suit, a light shirt and a dark, rich tie. This combination will bring people's eyes up to your face—your power look.

Several basic patterns exist in which you cannot go wrong. Any of these designs would make a proper tie for business or dressy occasions.

Rep Tie — Diagonal stripes of varying widths.

Club Tie — Small, spaced motifs or a solid color with one small motif in the center (a descendant of gentlemen's club ties).

Ivy League — Very small repeating pattern on solid ground.

Solid — Medium to dark silk or polyester.

| REP | CLUB | IVY LEAGUE | SOLID |

These tie patterns will give you a more casual look.

Knit — Knit or coarse weave.

Plaid Or Tweed — Basic large plaid or textured weave.

Paisley — Print of paisley design.

| KNIT | PLAID OR TWEED | PAISLEY |

HOW TO TIE THE BASIC TIE KNOTS

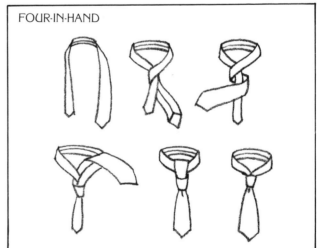

FOUR-IN-HAND

FITTING THE STYLE TO YOU

HALF WINDSOR

WINDSOR

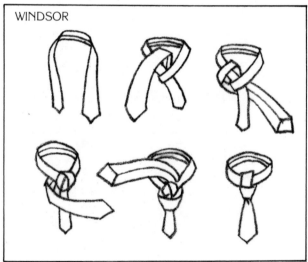

THE BOW TIE

A bow tie is slightly frivolous and fun. It enjoys the longest cycle in between periods of popularity of any fashion item we can name. For some men and in some circles, however, a bow tie for daytime wear makes a statement. Nonetheless, wearing a bow tie means that a lot of space between the collar and the belt is left unadorned, and that's why a bow tie is primarily put on for formal wear over a pleated or ruffled shirt.

The bow tie should be scaled to your face, its size suiting your face, neck and body proportion. The rules of fabric choice are similar to regular ties.

HOW TO TIE A BOW TIE

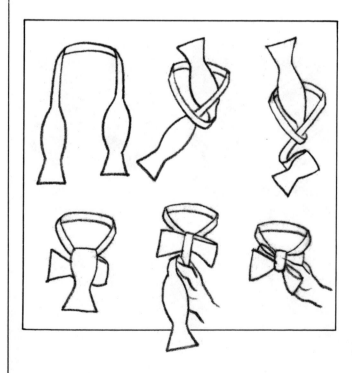

TIE TIPS

Length — Your necktie should end at the top of your belt. Anything longer or shorter looks tacky. Ideally, both ends should extend the same length, with the wide end just overlapping the narrow end. In practice this rarely happens because by the time you have found the perfect color, pattern and personality, who's going to quibble about length? For the record, however, you should know that a man:

5'7" and under	wears a	54" tie
5'8" to 6'	wears a	56" tie
6' and over	wears a	58" tie

Most men learn to adjust their ties so that the wide point reaches to the belt; then they do ingenious things with the smaller end. Shorter men tuck the span of extra length into the shirt between two buttons. Taller men have the narrow end riding near the chest. You should be aware that on the back of the wide end, every tie has a tab through which you can slip the narrow end so that both parts stay in place. That way, too, any discrepancy in length does not show.

A four-in-hand knot requires less length of tie than the bulkier Windsor knot. The type of knot you tie varies with the style of collar, width of suit lapel, whim of fashion and the fabric and construction of your tie. A silk tie is really the only type which can be worked into an acceptable Windsor knot.

Width — A classic tie width will run between 2-3/4 and 3-1/2 inches. A large man should tend toward a wider tie, while a smaller man will find better proportion with a narrower width. Check the tying portion of your tie. It should be about 1 to 1-1/4 inches wide.

The width of your tie must relate proportionately to the width of your suit lapel and to the size of your shirt collar. The wider the lapel, the wider the tie and the longer the collar points. Of great importance too is the size of your knot. A narrower tie needs a smaller knot to achieve a balanced proportion and a unified look.

Construction — A quality tie has good inner construction. The entire tie may be lined with silk, beneath which can be felt a strip of wool underlining. A tie of heavier fabric may use just the underlining. You don't need to be an expert in fabric and construction to develop a feel for a quality tie. The tie fabric should have good body, drape and flexibility while the lining and/or interfacing give it stability and character, especially in the neck area. Try on an expensive silk tie. Experience the ease of tying the knot, and appreciate the drape of the tie fabric. Then take this tip to heart: Economize on your underwear, not on your tie.

We know of a young couple who spent more money on a tie for the husband than the wife had ever paid for a blouse. They reeled from shock at first, but years later they realized that the precious tie proved to be one of the best clothing investments they had ever made.

FITTING THE STYLE TO YOU

CARE AND CLEANING OF TIES

Take care of every tie you own. After each wearing, untie the knot, give your tie a shake and then hang it on a tie rack. A knitted tie should be rolled up and stored in a drawer, as it tends to stretch.

Find a drycleaner who sends ties to a jobber specializing in them. A careless cleaning job will destroy silk ties.

Polyester ties wash beautifully in the gentle cycle of a washer and take just a few minutes in a cool dryer. If removed while still slightly damp, they may require no ironing. If you do press your ties, cut a cardboard insert to protect the front of the ties from markings imposed by construction of the back folds. Insert the cardboard at the tie's wide end, then press the front using a pressing cloth under the iron. A pocket handkerchief makes a good pressing cloth.

Wonderful polyester fabrics are available which look like silk. They will never have the elegant lustre or drape of pure silk, nor will they give you that extra boost of self-confidence — but for business and travel, and for men whose ties act as splashboards, they are a salvation.

No matter what the fabric, examine each tie to check for spots before you put it on. Nothing will blow your image faster than a dirty tie.

Remember, a tie is an expendable item and needs DISCARDING AND REPLACING REGULARLY.

Understanding what is best for your individual physique is only the beginning of clothing selection. Now it is time to consider what makes you so fascinating — your personality.

Personality

4

YOUR INDIVIDUAL CHARM

The most exciting men are those who have discovered who they are and feel comfortable with the knowledge. They see no need to apologize or boast, to make excuses or grandiose claims for themselves or their accomplishments. These men often show great personal style in their clothing and in the way they live. They do not necessarily qualify as fashion plates, but they have a way of wearing, say, a pair of faded jeans, an uncoordinated tennis outfit or a gray flannel suit which makes a definite statement about themselves and their lifestyle. What they have is "personal style."

How can you tell if you possess personal style or not? The determining factor is your ability to recognize and dress in harmony with your personality, and by that we mean the personality of appearance. This has nothing to do with whether you are a sinner or a saint—rather, your personality of appearance reflects the way other people see you. Personality of appearance is determined by your *coloring*, your *bone structure*, your *nervous system*, your *muscle tone*, your *fatty tissue* and your *environment*. You inherited the first four factors — coloring, bone structure, nervous system and muscle tone — and they cannot usually be altered. You cannot move your bones around, for example. In those respects, you are who you are. Fatty tissue, however, which you acquire all by yourself, can be changed. And so can your environment.

Actually, the influence works both ways — you can change your environment, and it can change you. Your appearance as a child

helped to shape your environment. If, when you were three, you looked five, your appearance affected the way you were treated and how you felt about yourself. If you were the smallest kid in your junior high, or the tallest, it had impact on your personality. If your muscle development lagged behind the growth of your bone structure, you might have been an awkward, somewhat clumsy adolescent. The quick, wiry kid with lots of nervous energy found himself a plague to teachers but a leader of his peer group. The child you were has shaped the man you are now.

Did you know that your coloring also influenced — and may still influence — the way people act toward you? A small blond child is treated differently than a wiry brunette. Redheads, blonds and brunettes have characteristic personalities because they grew up with those colorings and have been treated accordingly. Our society has been subconsciously conditioned to respond in certain ways toward certain types of appearance. If you are not convinced of this, think, if you will, when you ever saw a picture of a blond devil or a brunette angel.

We have discovered in our consultations with male clients that most of the top salesmen we meet are what we call Spring men, who are usually fair and blond. A Spring can sell anything. Few people hesitate to trust a blond, because he appears so guileless.

Discovering dimensions of your own personality can be both amusing and intriguing. While the following exercise is intended to help you choose clothing which

YOUR INDIVIDUAL CHARM

is more suited to you as an individual, you might also learn to understand and appreciate yourself better. If, as a side benefit, you also learn to understand and enjoy the qualitites and foibles of others a little more, then this book will have enriched your life.

YANG AND YIN THEORY OF PERSONALITY

In using the English language to describe people, we ran into a problem. So many words carry unfortunate connotations that we had to establish a vocabulary that would have less chance of offending our students. The major difficulty lay with ''masculine'' and ''feminine.'' Men and women have both feminine and masculine qualities, but our society has made us apprehensive about being labeled with these terms. Women don't like to be told they are masculine any more than men like to hear they have feminine traits. Yet men have qualities of gentleness, tenderness and nurturing just as women have qualities of independence, assertiveness and strength.

Adapting the theory of Yang and Yin to teach the concept of personality enabled us to evaluate the human qualities of an individual without threatening the ego.

The Yang and Yin symbol, found in all Oriental cultures, represents the balance between the contrasts found throughout the universe. We use this symbol as a teaching tool to help our students recognize and appreciate the balance of qualities in manner and appearance found in all well-adjusted adults. You will discover that you have qualities of both the Yang and the Yin — often at the same time — but one side will dominate. You may also learn that at different periods of your life, your dominant characteristics can change.

We have classified men's personality types into five categories: Dramatic, Natural, Classic, Romantic and Gamin. The Dramatic and Natural are the most Yang. The Classic and Romantic are the most Yin. The Gamin is a combination of the two. See PERSON—ALITY TYPES AND YANG AND YIN THEORY on pages 75 and 76.

It is possible to have a combination of Yin features and a Yang body or vice versa. A good example of this dichotomy was Hoss Cartwright (the late actor Dan Blocker) of the ''Bonanza'' TV show, who had a large Yang body and a Yin baby face. His big blue eyes and light coloring softened his Yang body.

On the other hand, Al Pacino of the movie ''The Godfather'' has a short Yin body and a strong, sophisticated Yang face with dark coloring. Dark coloring always adds sophistication and is Yang; light coloring appears more innocent and is Yin. This contrast is obvious in some Asian men who have small Yin bodies and large, dramatic Yang facial features.

Think of the five personality types as forming a continuum stretching from the extreme Yin to the extreme Yang. Your own personality will fall somewhere along the line. Your position on the continuum will vary at different times of your life and may take a different turn in the space of one day. Life situations and circumstances may push you one way or another, but eventually the real you will surface.

Compare your body type and behavior mannerisms with the PERSONALITY ANAL-YSIS CHART on pages 78 and 79.

Determine which personality or which combination of personality types most nearly describes you. After you have decided for yourself, have a family member or friend read the analysis and give you his or her opinion.

PERSONALITY TYPES

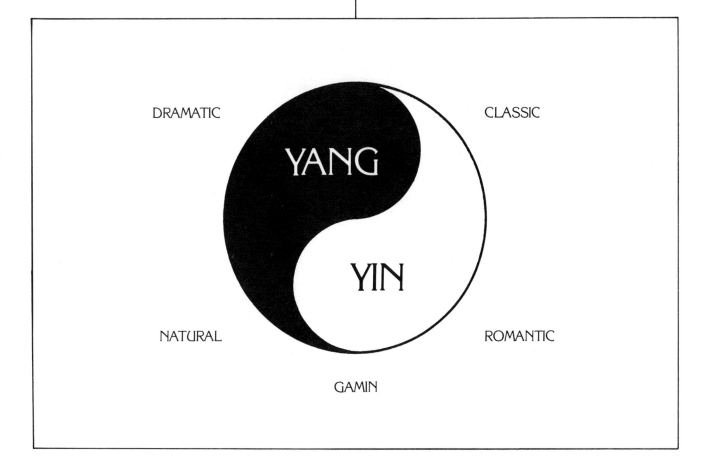

YOUR INDIVIDUAL CHARM

YANG AND YIN THEORY

YANG
Dark
Sun
Oak tree
Masculine
Dark hair
  or complexion
Large (bones or
  facial features)
Strong and sturdy
Mature
Sophisticated
Independent
Conservative
Pragmatic
Deliberate
Do·it·yourselfer
Gruff

YIN
Light
Moon
Willow tree
Feminine
Light hair
or complexion
Small (bones or
facial features)
Slim and thin
Youthful
Unsophisticated
Dependent
Flamboyant
Artistic
Spontaneous
Hire·it·done
Tender

DRAMATIC
Glen - Definite coloring, prominent facial features and a sophisticated high-fashion look identify the elegant Dramatic man.

NATURAL
Doug - Strong, sturdy, athletic, Doug is a typical Natural man. He has a square jaw and a friendly face with smiling eyes.

GAMIN
George - A sturdy, compact body and a friendly, capable, casual manner indicates a Gamin personality.

CLASSIC
Dallas - A look of serene self-control typifies the Classic man. His conservative dress and gentlemanly manner inspires confidence.

ROMANTIC
Bob - Attractive, flamboyant and appealing, the Romantic man has sex appeal.

YOUR INDIVIDUAL CHARM

	BODY TYPE	FACIAL FEATURES
DRAMATIC	Mature, medium to tall, angular. Can wear extreme fashions. Clothes horse.	Prominent, sharply defined features. Definite coloring. More often Winter season.
NATURAL	Average to tall in height. Strong, sturdy build, broad shoulders. Athletic appearance. Wholesome, outdoor type.	Broad or long face, square jaw. Tanned, freckled. Natural appearance. Friendly, smiling eyes. Approachable.
GAMIN	Small to medium height. Compact, coordinated. A small Natural. Could be slight or sturdy in build, but never large. Athletic appearance.	Open, friendly, happy face. Natural look, tanned or freckled. Mischievous sparkle in eyes. Rounded cheeks or chin, or a square jawline.
ROMANTIC	Any height, any build. Enjoys fine food and luxury. Could have tendency to be overweight.	Beautiful in a way unrelated to physical assets. Possesses a manner, an aura, a charisma that makes him attractive to women.
CLASSIC	Average to tall height, medium build. Balanced figure. Mature.	Regular features. Medium to light coloring. Rarely of sharp contrast, often Summer season.

HAIR STYLE	WALK AND GESTURES	BEHAVIOR	PROTOTYPES
Smooth, controlled. Professionally styled. Could have a lot of hair or none at all. Looks good in the "wet" look.	Poised, purposeful movements, firm and deliberate.	Sophisticated, self-assured, dignified, reserved. In control of self and situation.	George Hamilton, Ricardo Montalban, Harry Belafonte, Richard Gere, Jack Lord, Yul Brynner.
Windblown, casual. Could be bald.	Natural, casual, relaxed, energetic. Walks with a long free-swinging stride. Stands with hands on hips.	Friendly, frank, open. Talks with hands. Suffers from "foot in mouth." Voice is strong, clear, low-pitched. Always friendly. Comfortable.	John Wayne, Edward Kennedy, Robert Redford, O. J. Simpson, Merlin Olson, Tom Selleck Jack Klugman Jack Nicklaus
Natural, windblown, casual styles. Can wear the Afro hair style, a natural or a perm. Could be bald.	Quick, free-swinging walk. Natural looking. Talks with hands. Quick movements.	Alert, animated, enthusiastic. Young at heart. Friendly. Impatient, outspoken. Casual manner.	Johnny Carson, Dick Clark, Robert Conrad, James MacArthur, Sugar Ray Leonard, Bryan Gumble.
Controlled or uncontrolled. Straight or soft curls. Can wear hair longer, but it must be well groomed. Could be bald.	Relaxed, smooth, has rhythm. Affectionate in a comfortable, respectful way. His affection is genuine.	Likes women, makes them feel attractive. Charming. Can be flamboyant in dress, behavior or possessions and on him it looks good.	Sammy Davis, Jr., Omar Sharif, Burt Reynolds, Joe Namath, Robert Wagner, Mr. T.
Neat, controlled, conservative. Could be bald.	Poised, controlled, refined. Can move quietly to take charge of a situation.	Gentlemanly. Appears calm, in control. Reserved. Modulated voice.	Ronald Reagan, Paul Newman, Robert Young, John Forsythe, Richard Chamberlain, David Hartman

YOUR INDIVIDUAL CHARM

Most men are a composite of two or even three personality types. It is important to harmonize your various and sometimes differing qualities. This may be done by choosing outfits which avoid the extreme of any one personality and putting emphasis instead on the aspects of your individual coloring, facial expression and figure type which you yourself find most pleasing. In other words, if you feel you are a Natural-Romantic, you could dress in casual, relaxed-but-elegant Western wear during the day and go all out in a velveteen blazer, flannel slacks and silk shirt for evening. You can have the best of both worlds. Your Romantic side will dress up your Natural. Your Natural side will have a relaxing influence on your Romantic.

You may be able to identify your personality by reading the following descriptions and recognizing what kind of a wardrobe you already have or would like one day to own.

At any rate, don't waste your talents, strong points and energies in wishing you were different. Instead, find out just who you are and make the most of what you've got!
Dramatic

The Dramatic man could be described as an adult version of the Ivy League college student, suave, sophisticated and immaculately groomed. He wears European-styled suits; elegant, understated sportswear, such as cashmere sweaters; velveteen blazers; slacks rather than jeans; and evening attire is designed with him in mind. He can wear fads but avoids the outlandish, garish and anything in poor taste. A Dramatic man can wear an ascot scarf successfully. A single chain of medium size and of precious metal looks best around his neck. His ring would

be simple — a single diamond or ruby, set in an original design and in good taste.

The fabric of the Dramatic man's suits would be worsted wool, more likely plain than patterned. If pattern is used, it would be very muted, as in a faint chalk stripe, herringbone or a tone-on-tone plaid. He likes smooth cotton broadcloth for his shirts in a plain tone-on-tone or unobtrusive pattern, and he prefers silk ties with a lustrous finish.

His jogging suit would be velour, and his running shoes are clean. Whatever his taste in leisure activities, the Dramatic man has the proper clothes for them; he might never be seen in Levis. He wears pajamas for sleeping and owns an attractive bathrobe. He sends his shirts to the laundry. Because he takes excellent care of his clothes, they last a long time and retain the inimitable look of luxury even if he is not rich.

His hair is controlled and in place. If he wears a moustache or a beard, it is trimmed close and gives the impression of having been sculpted to his face.

The Dramatic man would prefer a larger luxury car, a larger dog and, if the fates allowed, a large bankroll would be convenient.

Natural

All men are Naturals to a degree. The qualities of independence and lack of concern about external appearance are an extension of the boy within all men.

The Natural man is casual and relaxed. His casualness should always be suggested by the design and cut of his clothing, even in formal wear. Because his body is likely to be sturdy, he looks for a straighter cut in jackets, less padding in the shoulders and an ample fit. These qualities in clothes accurately express his attitude about how he wants to dress—namely, for "comfort and utility."

Sportswear is the Natural's best look, and he should buy excellent quality. He needs an

expensive leather jacket (not suede), beautiful sweaters of every type, and fine polo and sports shirts. A snug fit in knitted shirts will accentuate good muscles. He should have beautiful, well-fitted slacks. The Natural man likes fabric with texture, but he should avoid corduroy because it always looks wrinkled.

YOUR INDIVIDUAL CHARM

He likes tweed, but if he is heavy he should choose a thinner, smoother tweed with only two colors. A slim Natural can wear heavy, coarse, multi-colored tweed if he likes the feel of it. The Natural man looks good with patches on the elbows of his jackets; patches will seem more elegant if the leather matches. The Natural enjoys fine gabardine and worsted wool in his suits, while he prefers wool of a softer feel or an interesting texture for sport coats. He loves camel's hair and cashmere. If he is stocky, he should avoid plaid in shirts, sport coats or suits unless the plaid is very muted. If the plaid is large or distinct, he'll look like a wall of plaid.

The Natural man should buy easy-care cotton-polyester shirts, avoiding 100% cotton shirts or silk shirts as they require professional care. Wool-and-polyester-blend suits and slacks resist wrinkles and look good on him in cool weather; in summer, he should wear cotton-polyester blends in slacks.

The Natural man dislikes being trussed up in a suit and vest. His idea of dress-up is an unbuttoned suit jacket, no vest, an ample-sized shirt and a loosened tie. He can carry off this look . . . if the clothes are of good quality and they are pressed.

The Natural man objects to jewelry, with the possible exception of a watch. He is the one who happily wears an enormous waterproof clock on his arm, but he should also own a second watch of sleeker dimensions for dress. He wouldn't be caught wearing a neck chain and wears rings only if they are hand-crafted and of sentimental value.

The Natural man is happiest wearing old, worn jeans and sweatshirts. He may be the finest skier on the slopes, but he'll never own a matching ski outfit. He bought his jacket last year, only to find that this year the color has gone out of fashion. Nonetheless, he often achieves great personal style with his haphazard combinations.

A man who sleeps in his skivvies and wraps himself in a towel, the Natural keeps his clothes forever and they fade to delicate hues. He is Mr. Clean. He washes his clothes but rarely has time to iron them because he is too busy waxing his skis, cleaning his rifle, sorting his tackle, waxing his surfboard, mending his wetsuit or washing his car.

The Natural's hair should be styled so that it does not require much combing. He can go without a shave (particularly if he is blond), wear dishevelled sports clothes, be covered with wholesome dirt and *still* look appealing.

If he is the cowboy type, he's set fashionwise because the Western look is accepted worldwide. He should keep his boots polished and his shirts tucked in, though. Unless he lives in cow country, however, he'll reserve his Western wear for his own free time.

The Natural man would rather own a good truck or a four-wheel-drive Jeep than a fancy car. He likes dogs and kids and tolerates women if they can cook. All he asks of life is to be able to earn enough money to enable him to play at his favorite games.

The Natural man can look rumpled and unkempt, or casual and classy—depending on the quality and care of the clothes he wears. Faded, well-worn but clean and pressed jeans paired with quality shoes, clean or polished, look terrific. Old jeans worn with disreputable shoes look tacky. He needs to discipline himself to take his clothes to the laundry or dry cleaner's because he'll never press them himself.

Gamin

The Gamin man is actually a combination of the Natural and the Romantic. Though shorter than the Natural, his build and personality are otherwise similar; in addition, he has much of the appeal and some of the flamboyance of the Romantic. A Gamin displays youthful qualities of enthusiasm and animation.

The Gamin man is the only type who wears the leisure suit successfully because of his compact, well-formed body. Good muscle development has less need for padding and inner construction in clothing.

In suits, he likes medium- to lightweight worsted woolens with good drape. He needs shaped suits. His slacks should be shaped above the knees to lengthen the legs. Happier than the true Natural with getting dressed up, he can even be a clothes horse. It is imperative for the Gamin man's clothes

to fit well. He usually needs the "short" sizes and youthful styling, so controlling his weight is an absolute must. He should use restraint in choosing patterned fabrics. He will look best in plain, heathered, muted small patterns, small tone-on-tone plaids or narrow pin stripes. Vests will lengthen his silhouette and give more of a power look for business. Light-colored dress shirts with a darker tie will draw a viewer's eye to the Gamin's face. The best shirt fabrics for him are broadcloth or Oxford cloth.

The Gamin man's sport coats and slacks should be of closely harmonizing colors for a taller look. Because of his good body proportion and muscle structure, he is great in sweaters of all types as long as they are not too bulky. He can wear natural or ethnic fabrics for casual wear. The Gamin man carries off all types of sports wear, both active and spectator, with flair. Shoes for business or dress wear should have a one-inch heel to give him added leg length.

The Gamin man needs jewelry of moderate size. A hand-crafted look in rings is best. He should avoid huge, bulky wrist-watches and wear a slim, plain, elegant watch for business or dress.

The Gamin man should strive for a snappy, young, contemporary look, avoiding anything flashy or extreme. Good quality and fit are the key. If a Gamin watches his weight and retains his muscle tone with regular workouts, he will be ageless.

Romantic

All men have a touch of Romantic reflected in their sincere affection, tenderness and caring.

The true Romantic is the flamboyant type who can wear all the outlandish things other men try to wear but can't get away with. He can sport several rings and elaborate chains with his shirt open to the waist and look fantastic. Super in shiny silk shirts, high fashion European-cut suits, turtleneck sweaters and a flower in his buttonhole, the Romantic man likes to dress up. He enjoys formal wear, vested suits and elegantly sexy casual wear. He is the type who would choose ruffled or tucked shirts for dressy occasions or formal wear. A clothes horse, the Romantic man will change outfits several times a day if the occasion warrants.

The Romantic needs to watch his weight and his muscle tone, or he will not be able to wear the slim-cut styles that fit his personality so well.

There is a fine line between elegant and cheap in the Romantic look. Because of the Romantic's love of extreme fashion, he may

go overboard; instead, he should use restraint and always opt for a more refined look. Nature has been very generous with the Romantic man; he has no need to gild the lily. He should wear his pants a little looser than he might otherwise, and perhaps leave

only three buttons undone on his shirt. As he matures, he needs to recognize when it is time to become more conservative in his dress. There is nothing sadder than a bechained, sagging, 50-year-old chest.

The Romantic should avoid heavy wing-tipped shoes and anything bulky, coarse or homespun. The Romantic man likes fine worsted wool and vests with his suits. He prefers silk ties and, for casual occasions, might wear silk shirts. If his body allows, he prefers as much shaping as possible in his suits. He likes camel's hair and cashmere sport coats; he might try velveteen for holiday flair, with superbly fitted slacks of lightweight worsted flannel or blue jeans and an open shirt. He wears designer jeans and the latest in sports attire, preferring smooth, silky fabrics for casual shirts and pure cotton polo shirts for relaxing. For dress shirts, he likes smooth, fine broadcloth or batiste. He would be inclined to send the whole lot to the cleaner's.

If the Romantic man uses patterned fabrics, the pattern will be subtle. He wears his clothes, they never wear him.

The Romantic man has sex appeal and he is very attractive to women. The world would be a duller place without him.

Classic

If a man matures gracefully in self-assurance and his interpersonal relationships, he will become more Classic. This quality of personality will be reflected in his grooming and his manner.

YOUR INDIVIDUAL CHARM

The Classic man's clothing should be essentially simple, dignified, fashionable but never faddish or severe. He enjoys wearing suits with vests. His suits can be styled with shaping or a straight cut, depending on his body. Because of his poise and control, he

can wear the double-breasted suit. Very conservative, the Classic man prefers plain fabrics, muted patterns, pin stripes or tone-on-tone glen plaids. He likes medium- to lightweight suit fabrics with a dull finish— never shiny. He dislikes tweed or rough or coarse textures. He could be the sweater-with-flannel-slacks type. His family should gift him with cashmere, however, because he'd never spend the money for it on himself.

The Classic man never throws anything away, so his leisure attire tends toward old trouser slacks and sweaters from his college days. He swears he has no need for good sportswear—swears it every week when an occasion occurs where he should wear it. He should buy at least one elegant sport coat of fine wool or Ultra Suede and two pairs of well-fitted wool slacks. He also needs a velour jogging suit, matching T-shirt and good tennis shoes. It is important for the Classic man to buy good quality because he is basically an elegant man.

His jewelry should be of a simple design, inconspicuous and of average size. He should avoid huge calender watches—he always knows what day it is anyway.

The Classic man is a bit of a penny-pincher. He doesn't want to spend a lot of money on clothes, but he can look very distinguished, successful and elegant. He needs good shoes, kept in good repair and polished well. He owes it to himself not to get into a rut with his wardrobe. The investment will be well worth it in terms of self-satisfaction and enjoyment.

The Classic's hair should be controlled. Though not necessarily limited as to its length, he should avoid extreme hair styles of any kind.

The Classic enjoys his home and is a traditional businessman. Professionally, he inspires respect and confidence, especially when he wears a look of success through good dressing. The Classic is well liked by his peers. He has a good shoulder for people to lean on. He may not play ball with his kids, but he will encourage them in all their endeavors.

PULLING IT ALL TOGETHER

To have personal style, you must be able to blend the Yang and Yin elements of your individual personality with the Yang and Yin elements in your clothes.

For example, if you are predominantly a Natural, that doesn't necessarily mean you should wear a ten-gallon hat like John Wayne. It suggests, though, that in attitude and personality you are less formal than men of other personality types. You will be happier than they would be — and feel more like yourself — in bolder, more rugged cuts, fabrics and colors. In working out your own wardrobe, you should lean toward the Natural athletic look.

To offer another example, the Classic man needs to recognize that his tendency for conservatism can make his wardrobe boring. He should balance his Classic aspect with the more relaxed Natural or the more dressy Romantic — whichever type he leans toward in his individual analysis.

When you listen to and look at what your body is telling you about your appearance and the texture, styling, comfort, fit and function of your clothes, you will understand the facets of your unique personality much better. Once you know who you are and what enhances your sense of self, you can develop the looks to complement your personality. Think about it, and then get on with analyzing your own individual lifestyle in order to plan a workable wardrobe.

Discovering Lifestyle 5

CLOTHES FOR THE LIFE YOU LEAD

There is a lot more to buying clothes than finding the right size. Clothes make up 90% of your appearance. They are the uniform by which you are judged, whether you like it or not. The initial impression you create with the right clothes and the image you maintain with an attractive wardrobe will have great influence on your success in the business world and in your social life.

Many men undercut themselves and cause others to under-value them because they wear rundown shoes, bad haircuts, and poorly chosen clothing. We have noted that when a man achieves a degree of success and has some discretionary cash, he invests it in a flashier car, a better camera or some fancy sporting goods, hardly ever thinking of getting a better looking suit. He forgets that his clothes convey his status to the world every day, while his expensive skis are stored away and the Porsche is parked out in the lot.

A man's position and self-image improve as he goes through life, but he is often slow to upgrade his clothing style accordingly. How do you really look to yourself? Does what you see reflect what you think of yourself or what you'd like others to think of you?

Dress standards vary from place to place. Because your ambition is to look good wherever you go, and you are trying to pull a workable wardrobe together as quickly as possible, the first rule you should follow is to stick to the classics. We lead you into classic, conservative clothes first because they are so versatile, forming the nucleus of any

wardrobe. They are easy to wear and stay in style. You can add flair to express your personality later.

In order for you to develop personal style, every outfit you acquire must be right for you in terms of its color and design as well as how it reflects your personality and lifestyle. A good wardrobe is built around your unique way of life, but lifestyles change from year to year. A change of employment, change of residence, your marital status, the growth of any children you might have and your age all influence your lifestyle and your clothing needs.

One of the notable gratifications in life is to be thought of by your peers as a well-dressed person. You will never gain that reputation by being the most casually dressed man at your place of business or at the activities you attend. If you want to be considered well-dressed, you must always wear outfits one level better than everyone else — not two levels better, or they'll hate you.

The trick is to observe carefully what your associates are wearing, socially or professionally, and then take the trouble to improve your own choices so that you always look just a little bit better than they do. Of primary importance, of course, is wearing the colors that are right for you. The rest of the technique is more subtle and has to do with the clothes themselves.

First of all, improve on the *type* of garment you wear. For example, at a casual gathering, everyone else may be wearing Levis and T-shirts; you wear slacks and a sport shirt. If they wear slacks and sport shirts, you wear slacks and a sport shirt, but wear a sport coat as well.

Secondly, improve on the *quality* of your outfits. You can achieve this with better fabrics, better tailoring, better fit and perfect accessories. If they wear polyester, you wear a natural fiber or a polyester that *looks* like a natural fiber. They may have lots of inexpensive clothes — you have a few excellent outfits.

Take note of those men in your profession or social group whose version of good dressing comes closest to your own intended look. Observe how such men meet needs similar to your own in the kinds of suits, shirts and shoes they wear and in the

I dunno, Lou . . . it just don't look the same!

length of their hair. The nature of your business may also affect your style choices. Bankers and lawyers, for example, tend to dress more conservatively than men in other professions, doubtless to enhance their credibility. Men in more flexible professions,

such as education, advertising, architecture, publishing and the like, have more leeway. Their clothing ranges from ultra-conservative classic suits to dressed-up blue jeans. Salesmen do well to fit in with their customers, but they should always display a look of success.

Pay attention to what's right for your own social community. Watch the men at your business association's social functions. Observe your local politicians, the president of the board of your local hospital or symphony committee. Who's who in your community? Look at what they wear and then gear those fashions to your age group and income level.

The fashion media are primarily concerned with reporting the latest fashion news and with creating lively photos. It is not always wise to buy according to the most recent editions, but glance through men's fashion magazines occasionally to see how the wind is blowing. Watch well-dressed men on current TV programs. Look, then decide, and always opt for the more conservative until you become a trend-setter yourself.

Remember: It is not the *quantity* that makes your reputation, it is the *quality*!

To know what you need in the way of clothes and accessories, you must analyze exactly where you normally go and what you do. Compiling a record of this information should be helpful. Most of the men we have counseled thought that they understood their clothing needs. The results of the following exercise, however, came as a revelation to them, as it probably will to you.

1. Keep a record of your clothing and activities for 24 hours a day. A well-dressed person is well dressed all the time. When we say "well dressed," we do not necessarily mean dressed up. We want you to be dressed in the best garment of its kind for the activity in which you are engaged. If you

CLOTHES FOR THE LIFE YOU LEAD

are painting the porch, you should be dressed for painting; but if you run out of thinner and have to dash to the store, you should change clothes. Why? Because if you don't, you are bound to meet half the people you know there; it's one of those perverse truths that the worse you look, the more acquaintances you'll meet.

2. Each day, write down where you went and what you wore. Then do some solid thinking and write down what you think would have been the best possible outfit you could have worn for that particular activity. For example, "Went to patio party at the Browns'. Wore jeans and my old Hawaiian print shirt. Wish I owned a good pair of slacks and a V-neck cashmere sweater."

3. Record any special needs you may have for occasions such as the company Christmas party, a cruise, vacations, etc.

4. Keep your daily record for three weeks. This period should cover most of the different places you go. If daily activities in the same clothes are repeated, record the outfit only once.

5. Repeat this exercise later in the year to make yourself aware of how your needs change with the climate.

6. Repeat this exercise every three to five years to keep abreast of changes in your lifestyle.

In three weeks, the third column on your recording chart will show you where your wardrobe is failing to work for you now in your current lifestyle. You might also list those activities which you would like to include in your future lifestyle.

WARDROBE PLANNING FOR MY LIFESTYLE 24 hours a day for 3 weeks 2 to 3 times a year every 3 to 5 years		
Where I Went	What I Wore	What I Wish I Had Worn

Artist, Graphics designer.

Part time university student and bus driver.

Latin charmer.

Full time father.

Leisure days a surf bum.

Weekdays an art broker.

CLOTHES FOR THE LIFE YOU LEAD

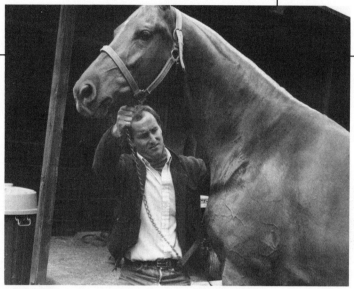

Actor, horseman, man-about-town.

Retired realtor – connoisseur.

Weekdays an office-bound dentist, holidays off to Hawaii.

Next, consider the following questions and the clothing you would need to enjoy an expanded way of life:

1. What are your cultural interests?
2. How do you entertain guests?
3. What sports interest you? Include both active and spectator sports.
4. What are your hobbies or special interests? What activities would you like to try?
5. Are you involved in your community?
6. Where do you spend your vacations?
7. Where would you *like* to spend your vacations?
8. Do your business and social lives overlap?
9. Do you travel in your business? If so, to what climate or part of the country?

Your WARDROBE PLANNING FOR MY LIFESTYLE chart and the answers to these questions will form the basis of a Priority Shopping Plan that you should start acting upon now. List the important purchases you wish to make as you begin to build your new wardrobe. You should have also discovered what items you need to round out the wardrobe you presently own.

CLEAR THE DECKS

The next assignment is a tough one, especially for men who hate to part with anything. But it's a vital preliminary move. Before you can get started building, you need to clean out your closet and drawers and get organized.

Plan a whole day for this onerous chore. Open your closet door and survey the accumulation of a lifetime: Shirts from your college days, suits from before you gained or lost weight 10 years ago, shoes with heavy soles and platform heels, and ties of every width, now limp and dingy with age. You are allowed to mourn and moan a little. Most closets are jammed with things which are never worn.

Start with the clothes. Take everything out and dump it on the bed. Sort your clothes into three piles according to the following chart:

ANALYSIS OF MY WARDROBE		
Wearables	Repairables	Discards

CLOTHES FOR THE LIFE YOU LEAD

WEARABLES

Everything that is ready to wear goes back into your closet. If the seams are intact, all the buttons are attached and the garment is clean, it is ready to wear, even if it is not your color. You may be able to put a better colored shirt with that wrong-colored sweater. No one can afford to discard good wearables. Wear them out or use them up until they can be replaced.

Once you've sorted out your wearables, there may not be many clothes left in your closet—how refreshing!

REPAIRABLES

A repairable is any item worth saving that is not immediately wearable. Pile your repairables wherever you put things in need of attention — those needing needlework in a spare closet — and those which are soiled in a pile to go to the dry cleaner or laundry.

DISCARDS

Those things in your closet which you have not worn for at least a year, with the exception of a tuxedo or other specialized garments, discard or donate to your favorite charity. Chances are that you will never lose

those extra pounds. Those ties are beyond reclamation. If you are waiting for wide, peaked lapels to be resurrected, forget it! The silhouette might return, but something will be different — the emphasis of fit, the shoulder pads, or something else. If you find good shirts you have not worn for a year, you either have too many shirts or not enough slacks to go with them.

Repeat the discard process with your shoes, belts, socks and handkerchiefs. Place the tie from Aunt Lucy and the one from your old school — ties you just can't part with — into a shoebox labeled "Old Ties" and store it at the top of your closet.

MAKE A LIST

From those few lonely clothes that remain hanging, uncrushed, in your closet, cut a fabric sample out of a seam allowance or hem. On a large safety pin, collect these swatches of your clothes. This is your wardrobe record to carry when you go shopping, to help you match and coordinate possible purchases. We urge you to do this because 20 seconds after you turn your back on a color, you cannot remember its exact shade. Your safety pin full of fabric pieces serves as your color and texture reminder. As you purchase subsequent garments—suits, slacks and sport coats—if you have any tailoring done, ask for any scraps or bits of fabric the tailor might cut off. Add a scrap of each new purchase to your safety pin. Carrying clothes around a shopping center for matching is irksome and tiring. With your safety pin full of your fabric scraps and your color palette in your hand, coordinating your clothing is easy.

List the wearables you have in your wardrobe and note any new purchases you might want to make. Add these items to your Priority Shopping List, and you'll be on your way with a workable wordrobe plan.

"Please deposit another fifteen cents!"

Planned Shopping 6

PROTECTING YOUR INVESTMENT

With the escalation of clothing prices, men have no choice but to become cost-conscious consumers. You must acquire shopping expertise, techniques of which most men are woefully ignorant, and gain at least a nodding acquaintance with the facts of garment manufacture, merchandising, fabric and maintenance. Your first shopping trip after reading this book should not be to buy, but to discover your options. Dress in your best and go conquer the territory.

Should you shop at a big department store or a smaller shop? Each has advantages and problems. The difference between a department store and a small shop boils down to the fact that in a small shop the owner or manager is running the business and has a big stake in keeping you well satisfied so that you'll come back, while the average department store clerk is holding down a job and to him or her, one customer is as good as another. Your choice is determined by where you get the best service and the best buys for your money.

MIND YOUR MONEY

Time is money in shopping. Find the stores that specialize in merchandise suited to your individual needs, where the buyer's taste coincides with your taste, your age and your wallet. Learn to recognize those places which emphasize good taste. Spend some time there, even if you cannot hope to buy, so that you get a feel for quality and lasting fashion as opposed to fad merchandise. This kind of research takes an objective attitude.

"Is not to worry, Joe . . . pin stripes are back!"

Walk into the store and observe the decor, the displays, the type and price of merchandise, even the age and dress of the sales personnel and their attitudes, to get a feel for the type of man this business is trying to attract.

Some stores specialize in volume merchandising and can offer good buys in basic needs such as socks and underwear.

PROTECTING YOUR INVESTMENT

Drop into a luxury shop and try on a few very expensive suits and jackets to get a feel for quality. Consider the staying power of the style and garment's wearability in relation to its original price and the cost of upkeep. This is of particular importance when buying light colors or fragile fabrics. Special handling by your dry cleaner can be very expensive.

By trying on a variety of clothes from different cutters, you can get an idea of the size range you require for comfort and wearability, and you'll recognize that size varies with different manufacturers. You are fortunate if you have a lady in your life who enjoys shopping. Take her with you on this familiarization excursion. If she learns your colors and your size range, and she understands your needs and your tastes, she can act as a scout later when you are planning a purchase. She might discover a coat in one store and a suit in another worthy of consideration, and guide you to them without your having to visit every store in town.

DEPARTMENT STORES

Quantity buying by department stores can make prices more reasonable there as compared to custom shops. Because plenty of floor space is available, department stores offer a wider selection of styles. Returns are easily and pleasantly made. A reputable department store stands behind its merchandise: Defective garments will be sent back to the manufacturer, while returns for other reasons are handled with a minimum of fuss and bother. Just remember, all department stores buy from the same sources, so they may all carry the same merchandise.

SMALL SHOPS

Small shops may offer you specialized service, and the atmosphere is often pleasant and unique. In well-run small shops, you get personal attention. Wise shop owners are interested in making a sale, of course, but they are even more interested in gaining a steady customer. Small shops usually specialize in a certain type of clothing keyed to a particular type of man. It is easy to exchange or get credit for returned merchandise but often difficult to get cash refunds. Always ask about store policy before making your purchase.

LABELS

Read labels carefully for information as to the fiber content. You must know what you've got before you can have a garment cleaned or washed, or even decide whether you can store it without mothballs.

Each manufacturer or cutter has a particular body type in mind when he or she makes clothes. All of his or her garments are cut from the same master pattern. For example, if a size 40 Pierre Cardin suit fits you perfectly, then all Pierre Cardin suits of the same size will fit you. Find the cutter of suits, shirts or slacks who has *you* in mind.

A large store might have clothes from several manufacturers on its racks. If you discover a garment which fits you perfectly, find out who made it. The store label will give no indication, but a helpful manager can tell you. You could even write to the cutter to discover what other stores carry his or her line. Once you found out, it would be the next best thing to having your own tailor.

QUALITY

Plan your purchase of more costly garments such as suits and coats for different times, to spread out the impact on your budget. Buy the best you can afford. Never count the cost of a garment or accessory—it is the *cost-per-wearing* that counts. A classic worsted wool suit, worn five years, is a better buy than a polyester suit which might look tacky after one year. Quality usually means economy in the long run. Buy more non-seasonal than seasonal clothing. And in every case, evaluate the garment in terms of good design, lasting fashion, durability of fabric, ease of care and its suitability to you and your way of life.

BUYING AT SALES

If service is what you want, then forget about sale buying. But if you know the merchandise and are familiar with name-brand manufacturers, a sale can be a worthwhile experience.

There are two ways to shop at a clearance: Early for the cream or late for the drippings. Be aware that many stores import inferior or old merchandise for a sale, and beware of wholesale or outlet buying unless your connections are very good indeed.

SPEND YOUR MONEY WHERE IT COUNTS

Learn to judge fashion, appreciate quality, and take care of your clothes. A good press, polished shoes and a flair with accessories can make a mediocre garment look terrific. Buy clothes for your lifestyle. *Spend the most money where you spend the most time.*

Be vain about your good points and make the most of them. Keep your figure challenges a secret by choosing clothes to conceal them. Use color to flattering advantage. Dress to suit the occasion. If you are not sure what to wear and can't ask someone, always opt to be a little over-dressed rather than underdressed. Keep within your budget. It is not always how much you spend that makes you well dressed, but how wisely and tastefully you spend it.

Remember that "ready-to-wear" is a term that should apply to everything you own. Always have your clothes clean and well pressed. Every personal appearance is an important one.

SHOPPING LAWS

1. Shop alone or with someone who is objective about your needs, your colors, your style and your personality.

2. Dress well when shopping to gain respect from salespeople.

3. Decide what you really need and put first things first. Use your Priority Shopping List to control impulse buying and develop sales resistance.

4. Forget all of your preconceived ideas about color. Decide which of your neutrals you want to start with and then carry out your plan.

5. Shop for your colors during your own season's time of year. This applies primarily to sport and casual clothes. For example, polo shirts in Spring's colors are available in the spring of the year.

6. Consider each purchase in this order: Size, color, line, texture, fit and personality.

7. If you are not happy and confident about your purchase, *don't buy it!*

FIBER AND FABRIC—FACTS FOR MEN

In order to be a careful consumer, you need a little nontechnical information about fabric, its construction or weave and its fibers.

PROTECTING YOUR INVESTMENT

Weave — Fabrics normally found in clothing are either woven or knitted. Knits are of loopy construction and will stretch to varying degrees providing comfort and resistance to wrinkling. Woven fabrics are rigid. Garments made of woven fabrics depend on styling and good fit for comfort. Their resistance to wrinkles is dependent on the type or quality of the fiber used in construction. Practically all clothing for active sportswear, such as sweatshirts, warm-up pants and all their derivatives, are made of *knitted fabrics.* T-shirts and their dressier descendants, swim wear, ski wear, sweaters and socks are made of knitted fabrics as well. The very thing that enables knit to perform so marvelously for active wear precludes its successful use in any garment, such as a suit, which depends for its appearance on the stability of the fabric. Polyester double-knit suits hit the market and every man bought *one,* discovered its shortcomings and never bought another. Cutters responded to consumer resistance, and we rarely find a knitted suit today. Knitted suits and slacks lost their shape and snagged. The snagging was due to the polyester fiber, incidentally, and not to the knit construction of the fabric.

Men who travel find that double-knit slacks are extremely comfortable and marvelously resistant to wrinkles. Double-knit is a heavier fabric, as its name implies, having less stretch and more suitability for outerwear such as suits and slacks. The only objection is that the polyester knit still snags and tends to cling to the body unless it is of excellent quality. If you buy polyester double-knit slacks, use great caution in your choice of fabric design as well as quality. Choose understated patterns similar to those found in expensive worsted wools. Avoid flashy plaids or any design which includes vivid contrasting colors or tones.

"...and it comes with its own little box of checkers!"

Suits, coats, slacks, dress shirts and the vast majority of fabrics with which we come in contact are *woven fabrics*—found in upholstery, drapery, sheets and blankets. Depending on how closely the fibers are woven, the fabric will be strong and stable. In menswear, the design is usually woven into the fabric; however, fabrics for sport shirts, beach wear, etc. may be printed.

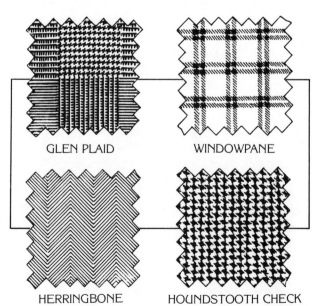

GLEN PLAID   WINDOWPANE

HERRINGBONE   HOUNDSTOOTH CHECK

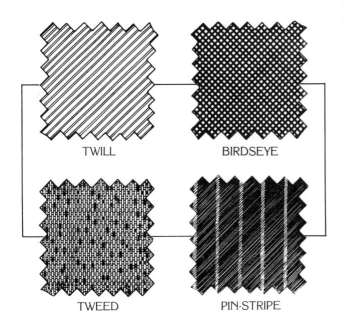

TWILL BIRDSEYE

TWEED PIN-STRIPE

Fiber — It is no accident that designers work primarily with natural fibers, for fabrics made of natural fibers like cotton, wool and silk work well into clothing. They can be steamed, eased and molded into shape. Synthetic or man-made fabrics such as nylon, acrylic and polyester are harder to work with.

Natural fibers breathe, which means they have the ability to absorb body moisture and then transport it to the outside of the fabric where it can evaporate. Perspiration and body oils will dry-clean or wash out of natural fibers. Polyester and nylon, on the other hand, have a tendency to grab grease-spots and body oils and to retain perspiration odor. When you wash such fabrics, try a final rinse in a basin of water to which you have added a couple of teaspoonsful of either ammonia or vinegar to combat the odor.

Natural fibers wear longer and are not subject to abrasion. In contrast, synthetic fibers wear at every seam, collar roll and cuff edge. Synthetics are particularly sensitive to heat and will melt or glaze under the temperature of a domestic iron if not protected with a pressing cloth.

Natural fibers also take dye better, allowing for clear, vivid and ice tones. Synthetics will not take a true jet black, for example, and tend toward muted tones in other colors. This is the reason that Winter is said to be the "expensive season," because good Winter colors are more often found in silk, cotton and wool which take clear dyes and are inevitably more expensive.

We don't mean to knock man-made fibers, however. With continued research, synthetics improve each year. It is hard to imagine living without them. At this writing, the most effective use of synthetic fibers seems to be in blends with natural fibers — that way you get the best of both worlds. The finest suits, however, are almost always made of 100% pure worsted wool.

Natural Fibers:

Worsted Wool — This fabric is made from the long fibers of wool. Usually closely woven, it offers the most in comfort, wrinkle resistance and long wear. Because it has a hard finish, worsted wool resists lint. It tailors beautifully and is the most expensive.

Wool — This term is used for fabric made of the shorter wool fibers. Wool can be of excellent quality; it tailors well, wears well and creates a softer finish than worsted.

Virgin Wool — means a new wool, never used before. This term on a label provides no guarantee of quality.

Reprocessed Wool — is wool obtained from products previously manufactured, but never used or worn. Less warm than virgin wool and of a harsher texture, reprocessed wool is rarely used for clothing.

Cotton — This fiber provides maximum warm-weather comfort; it is often found in blends with polyester. Shirts of 100% cotton usually require ironing, a skill most people have happily forgotten. If you are not inclined to drop your shirts off at the laundry, you would be wiser to choose a cotton/polyester blend which is easy to care for.

PROTECTING YOUR INVESTMENT

Silk — This is the strongest of the natural fibers, creating a very comfortable and elegant fabric. Found in blends in men's suiting, it adds lustre. It is best used in neckties. For silk to have an appreciable effect on the strength or function of a fabric, it must comprise at least 25% of the fiber. A much smaller percentage can have effect on the appearance, however.

Linen — This fiber offers the ultimate in warm-weather comfort, also the ultimate in wrinkle collection. It is an expensive wrinkle, too. Found in blends in men's suiting, linen adds interest to the fabric, and in blends it has less tendency to wrinkle.

Man-Made Fibers:

Polyester — This fiber is found in knits and woven fabrics in men's suits and slacks. With its tendency to snag and bag, polyester has a limited life span. Suits and slacks of this fiber lose the new look after several seasons' wear; however, garments will retain their new look longer if they are dry-cleaned. Polyester is most successfully used in blends. In shirts of polyester and cotton, you get the best of both fibers.

Nylon — This fiber resembles silk, especially DuPont's Quiana. Nylon offers little in comfort, but much in its ease of care and resistance to wrinkles.

Acrylic or Orlon — This fiber most nearly resembles the wool fiber. It takes a brilliant dye, but it also "pills," that is, it develops tiny balls of fiber, and loses shape. Most often found in sweaters and athletic sweats, acrylic is not suitable for slacks. It will retain its new look longer if it is dry-cleaned.

Rayon or Acetate — In menswear, this fiber is most usually found as a lining or in a blend, where it adds wrinkle resistance. If a polyester garment is lined with rayon or acetate, it should be dry-cleaned, never washed. Rayon, acetate or triacetate offer more moisture absorption than other man-made fibers.

CARE AND CLEANING OF CLOTHING

Allow your suits and wool garments to rest for 24 hours between wearings to allow their fibers to regain resiliency. If your clothes have been worn in smoke-filled rooms, let them air out before hanging them in your closet. Empty all pockets and hang your jackets, unbuttoned, on thick wishbone-shaped wooden hangers. For pants, empty the pockets, leave the fly unzipped and remove the belt before hanging them over a wooden hanger with a crossbar dowel thick enough not to crease the legs. Don't pack your closet with garments — an overcrowded closet is hard on wool clothes. Wool benefits from circulation of air.

Sponge off spots and restore the creases in your garments with an iron and a pressing cloth to lengthen the period between cleanings. Use a dependable dry cleaner. Even the best quality dry cleaning is hard on clothes because it wears down the fibers. Always dry clean all parts of a suit together to avoid color mismatching. Never wear suit pants without the jacket; have extra slacks for casual wear. When suits, jackets and pants return from the cleaner's, switch them immediately to their own thick hangers.

Before you put shirts and other washables in the machine, pretreat heavily soiled areas such as collars, cuffs or any spots with Spray and Wash™ or any popular pretreating solution. Wash dress shirts, underwear and lightly soiled clothes no longer than eight minutes in the wash cycle — any longer and you will merely be wearing them out.

Set a timer and remove cotton-polyester blend shirts from the dryer while still warm and slightly damp. Place them on hangers and they will need little ironing.

Half the battle in being well dressed is taking good care of your clothes. The finest and most expensive garments cannot withstand abuse, while those of less quality will be much improved by careful cleaning and pressing. Develop a caring attitude about your clothes as you begin to formulate your wardrobe plan.

Dress Suit or power look for business
Suit; dark navy worsted
Shirts; white, ice pink or ice blue
tone-on-tone
Tie; navy with red polka dots

Business Suit
Suit; blue with red glen plaid
Shirt; blue
Tie; maroon with white dots

Business Suit
Suits; gray herringbone worsted
Shirt; white
Tie; black with red and white dots

Business Suit
Suit; gray worsted
Shirts; white broadcloth or blue oxford
Tie; gray and blue wide stripe

Sport Coat
Jacket; maroon flannel
Slacks; gray flannel
Shirt; white broadcloth
Tie; maroon and gray stripe

WINTER WARDROBE COMBINATIONS

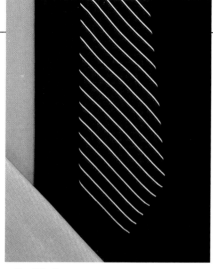

Sport Coat
Jacket; navy blazer
Slacks; taupe worsted
Shirt; blue oxford
Tie; navy with red and taupe stripe

Sport Coat
Jacket; spruce (blue-green) flannel
Slacks; blue-green herringbone
Shirt; ice aqua
Tie; blue-green with dots

Sport Coat
Jacket; black, gray and white houndstooth
Slacks; black gabardine or gray flannel
Shirt; white or gray
Tie; black with gray and white stripe

Sport Coat
Jacket; navy blazer
Slacks; navy, green, white and yellow plaid
Shirt; white broadcloth
Ties; navy and green with yellow stripes,
yellow knit

Dress Suit or power look for business
Suit; blue and plum heathered flannel
Shirts; pale violet, pink or blue
Tie; blue, plum and mauve stripe

Business Suit
Suit; blue-gray worsted
Shirts; off-white or gray broadcloth or blue oxford
Tie; blue and red stripe

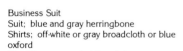

Business Suit
Suit; blue and gray herringbone
Shirts; off-white or gray broadcloth or blue oxford
Tie; blue, gray and white print

Business Suit
Suit; blue glen plaid
Shirt; gray broadcloth
Tie; blue linen solid

Dress or Business Suit
Suit; blue heathered flannel
Shirt; gray broadcloth
Tie; burgundy club

Wardrobe Combinations continued on page 112.

WINTER COLOR PALETTE

The true basic primary colors.
The key to your color selection is true or blue and clear. True red,
blue-red; true green, blue-green; true blue, blue-blue; true gray, blue-gray, etc.

USE OF COLOR

Neutral Colors are the chalk-white, true or blue-grays, black, navy and gray-beiges. They are basic and will go any place, any time. Neutral colors are most elegant when harmonized with hair and/or eyes. When you are tired, wear a colored shirt with your neutrals to give you a lift.

Basic Colors are the true or blue-reds, blues and greens, in your medium to dark shades. They will go most any place, any time. They are very becoming because they add color to your face. Basic colors are mixed with neutrals in men's suiting.

Bright Colors are the more intense, medium to dark shades. Use them as bright accents with neutrals or mix in prints. They are fun colors for active sportswear. Bright shirts should not be worn with suits for business.

Light Colors give a dressier look in shirts for business and formal wear. They can be used for sweaters, summer suits, sports wear or pajamas.

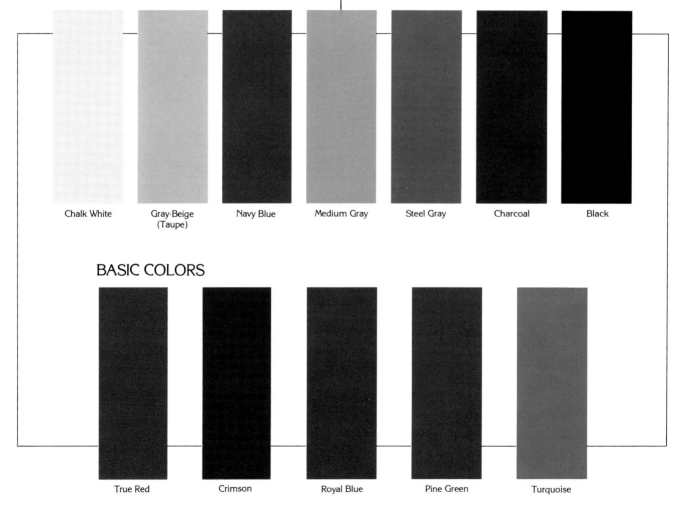

NEUTRAL COLORS

| Chalk White | Gray-Beige (Taupe) | Navy Blue | Medium Gray | Steel Gray | Charcoal | Black |

BASIC COLORS

| True Red | Crimson | Royal Blue | Pine Green | Turquoise |

104

BRIGHT COLORS

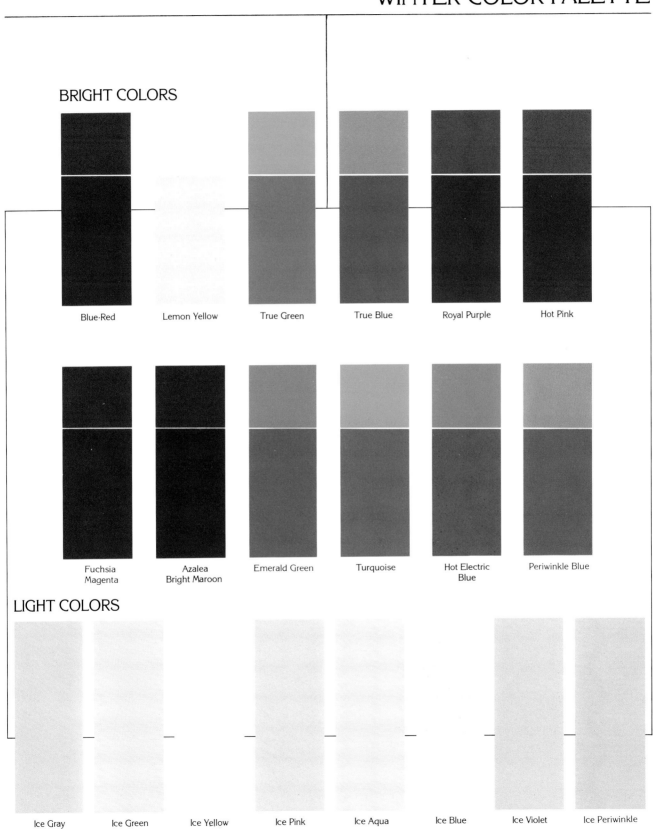

Blue-Red   Lemon Yellow   True Green   True Blue   Royal Purple   Hot Pink

Fuchsia Magenta   Azalea Bright Maroon   Emerald Green   Turquoise   Hot Electric Blue   Periwinkle Blue

LIGHT COLORS

Ice Gray   Ice Green   Ice Yellow   Ice Pink   Ice Aqua   Ice Blue   Ice Violet   Ice Periwinkle

SUMMER COLOR PALETTE

Muted shades of blue or rose undertone.
When your colors are medium to light they can be muted or clear. When they are from medium to dark,
they should be muted. Bright intense colors will wear you.

USE OF COLOR

Neutral Colors are off-white, blue-gray, gray-navy, rose-beige and rose-brown. They are basic and will go any place, any time. Neutral colors are most elegant when harmonized with hair and/or eyes. When you are tired, wear a colored shirt with your neutrals to give you a lift.
Basic Colors are the blue-reds, gray blues and blue-greens, in your medium to dark shades. They will go most any place, any time. They are very becoming because they add color to your face. Basic colors are mixed with neutrals in men's suiting.

Bright Colors are the more intense, medium to dark shades. Use them as bright accents with neutrals or mix in prints. They are fun colors for active sportswear. Bright shirts should not be worn with suits for business.
Light Colors give a dressier look in shirts for business and formal wear. They can be used for sweaters, summer suits, sports wear or pajamas.

NEUTRAL COLORS

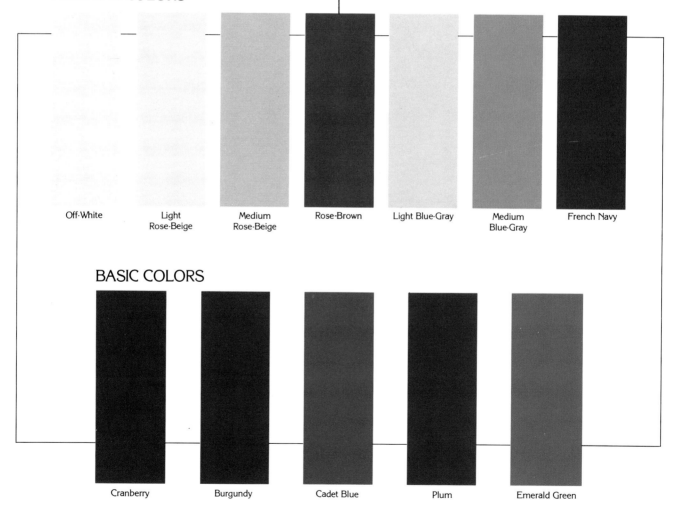

| Off-White | Light Rose-Beige | Medium Rose-Beige | Rose-Brown | Light Blue-Gray | Medium Blue-Gray | French Navy |

BASIC COLORS

| Cranberry | Burgundy | Cadet Blue | Plum | Emerald Green |

BRIGHT COLORS

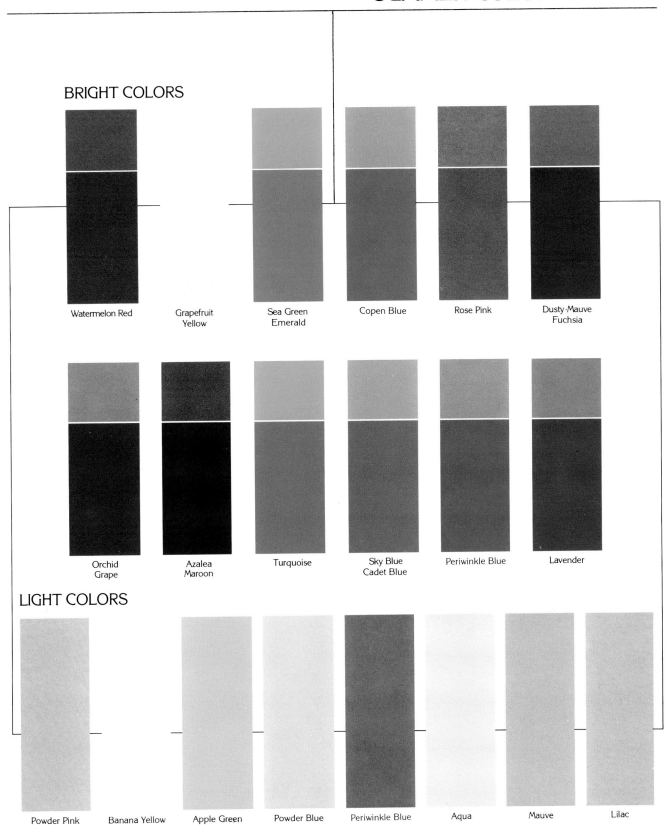

Watermelon Red

Grapefruit
Yellow

Sea Green
Emerald

Copen Blue

Rose Pink

Dusty-Mauve
Fuchsia

Orchid
Grape

Azalea
Maroon

Turquoise

Sky Blue
Cadet Blue

Periwinkle Blue

Lavender

LIGHT COLORS

Powder Pink

Banana Yellow

Apple Green

Powder Blue

Periwinkle Blue

Aqua

Mauve

Lilac

SPRING COLOR PALETTE

Yellow undertone, warm, clear, fresh fruit, spring bouquet colors.
Spring has the greatest range of colors of any season. Your only limitation is that
you cannot successfully wear colors much darker than the selection in your color deck.

USE OF COLOR

Neutral Colors are the warm whites, warm grays, clear royal navy, warm golden beiges and golden-browns. They are basic and will go any place, any time. Neutral colors are most elegant when harmonized with hair and/or eyes. When you are tired, wear a colored shirt with your neutrals to give you a lift.

Basic Colors are the clear yellow-reds, clear blues, clear yellow-greens, and clear golds in your medium shades. They will go most any place, any time. They are very becoming because they add color to your face. Basic colors are mixed with neutrals in men's suiting.

Bright Colors are the more intense, medium to dark shades. Use them as bright accents with neutrals or mix in prints. They are fun colors for active sportswear. Bright shirts should not be worn with suits for business.

Light Colors give a dressier look in shirts for business and formal wear. They can be used for sweaters, summer suits, sports wear or pajamas.

NEUTRAL COLORS

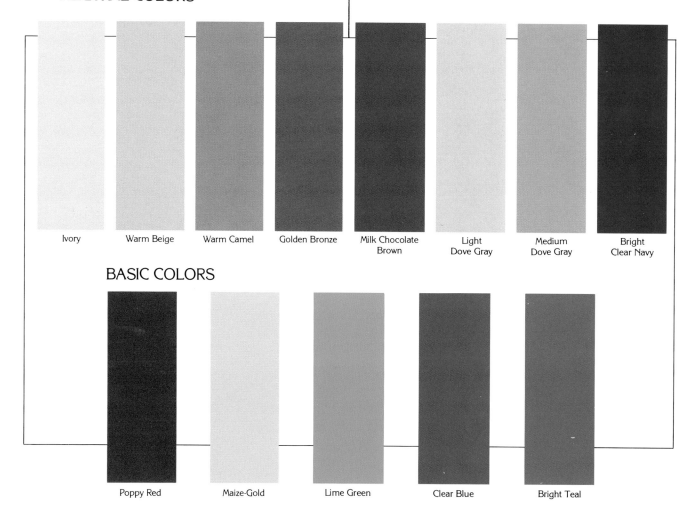

| Ivory | Warm Beige | Warm Camel | Golden Bronze | Milk Chocolate Brown | Light Dove Gray | Medium Dove Gray | Bright Clear Navy |

BASIC COLORS

| Poppy Red | Maize-Gold | Lime Green | Clear Blue | Bright Teal |

BRIGHT COLORS

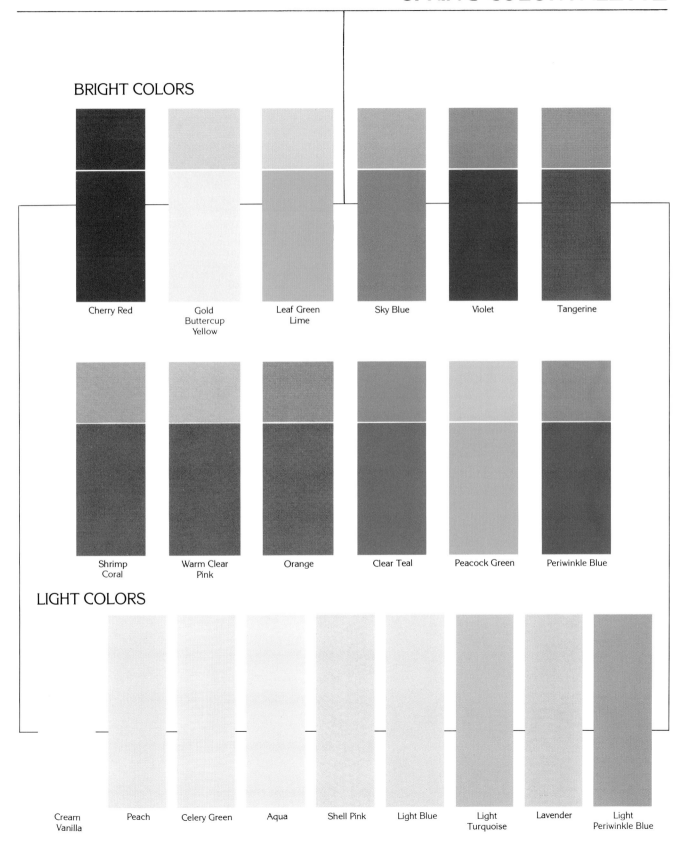

Cherry Red

Gold
Buttercup
Yellow

Leaf Green
Lime

Sky Blue

Violet

Tangerine

Shrimp
Coral

Warm Clear
Pink

Orange

Clear Teal

Peacock Green

Periwinkle Blue

LIGHT COLORS

Cream
Vanilla

Peach

Celery Green

Aqua

Shell Pink

Light Blue

Light
Turquoise

Lavender

Light
Periwinkle Blue

AUTUMN COLOR PALETTE

Yellow undertones;
earthy, muted shades and colors
of metal and wood.

USE OF COLOR

Neutral Colors are the warm whites, warm beiges and warm browns. They are basic and will go any place, any time. Neutral colors are most elegant when harmonized with hair and/or eyes. When you are tired, wear a colored shirt with your neutrals to give you a lift.
Basic Colors are the yellow-reds, teal-blues, yellow-greens and golds, in your medium to dark shades. They will go most any place, any time. They are very becoming because they add color to your face. Basic colors are mixed with neutrals in men's suiting.

Bright Colors are the more intense, medium to dark shades. Use them as bright accents with neutrals or mix in prints. They are fun colors for active sportswear. Bright shirts should not be worn with suits for business.
Light Colors give a dressier look in shirts for business and formal wear. They can be used for sweaters, summer suits, sports wear or pajamas.

NEUTRAL COLORS

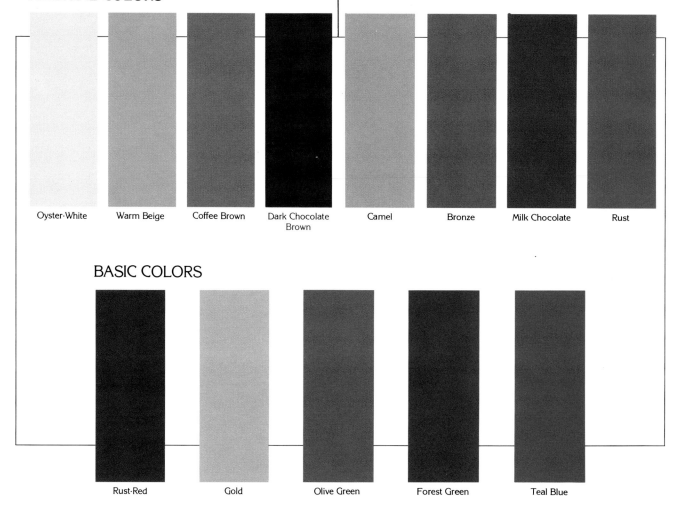

| Oyster-White | Warm Beige | Coffee Brown | Dark Chocolate Brown | Camel | Bronze | Milk Chocolate | Rust |

BASIC COLORS

| Rust-Red | Gold | Olive Green | Forest Green | Teal Blue |

BRIGHT COLORS

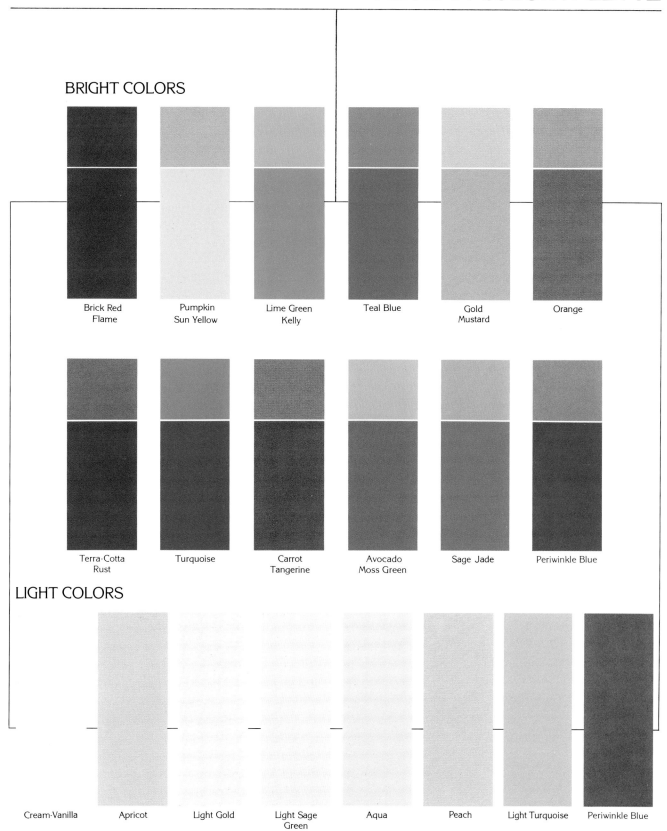

| Brick Red Flame | Pumpkin Sun Yellow | Lime Green Kelly | Teal Blue | Gold Mustard | Orange |

| Terra-Cotta Rust | Turquoise | Carrot Tangerine | Avocado Moss Green | Sage Jade | Periwinkle Blue |

LIGHT COLORS

Cream-Vanilla   Apricot   Light Gold   Light Sage Green   Aqua   Peach   Light Turquoise   Periwinkle Blue

SUMMER WARDROBE COMBINATIONS

Sport Coat
Jacket; blue-green glen plaid
Slack; blue-green flannel
Shirts; off-white or aqua
Tie; blue-green with gray dot

Sport Coat
Jacket; burgundy glen plaid flannel
Slacks; burgundy heathered flannel or
rose-beige gabardine
Shirts; off-white broadcloth or mauve
oxford
Tie; burgundy club

Business or Casual Suit
Suit; rose-brown twill
Shirt; pink
Tie; burgundy with rose and beige stripe

Sport Coat
Jacket; burgundy flannel
Slacks; light burgundy heathered flannel
Shirt; off-white
Tie; burgundy with stripes

Dress Suit or power look for business
Suit; navy worsted
Shirt; cream broadcloth
Tie; blue and red stripe

Business Suit
Suit; brown glen plaid
Shirts; cream, beige or peach broadcloth
or blue oxford
Tie; brown with blue, peach and white
stripe

Suit; dove gray gabardine
Shirts; off-white, gray or blue
Tie; blue, gray and white print

Business Suit
Suit; blue and tan glen plaid
Shirts; tan broadcloth or blue oxford
Tie; blue and tan paisley

Business Suit
Suit; milk chocolate worsted
Shirts; beige or peach broadcloth or blue
oxford
Tie; brown multi-colored stripe

SPRING WARDROBE COMBINATIONS

Sport Coat
Jacket; gray and navy tweed
Slacks; navy or gray gabardine
Shirts; off-white broadcloth or blue oxford
Tie; Spring blue linen

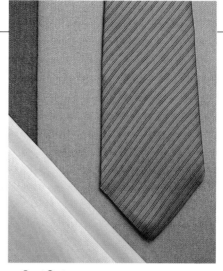

Sport Coat
Jacket; camel flannel
Slacks; turquoise heathered flannel
Shirts; beige, yellow or aqua broadcloth
Tie; camel with blue and gold stripes

Sport Coat
Jacket; camel herringbone
Slacks; milk chocolate or camel flannel
Shirts; off-white, peach or yellow
Tie; brown multi-color stripe

Sport Coat
Jacket; camel flannel
Slacks; camel, blue and gold plaid
Shirt; beige
Tie; yellow knit

Dress Suit or power look for business
Suit; dark chocolate worsted
Shirt; off-white tone-on-tone
Tie; brown with stripes

Business Suit
Suit; brown glen plaid
Shirts; beige or peach broadcloth
Tie; brown with rust dots

Business Suit
Suit; coffee flannel
Shirt; beige or aqua
Tie; brown plaid

Sport Coat
Jacket; beige and brown tweed
Slacks; dark chocolate gabardine or rust flannel
Shirts; beige or pink
Tie; brown, rust and cream stripes

Business Suit
Suit; brown muted glen plaid
Shirts; off-white with brown stripe or blue oxford
Tie; brown club

Sport Coat
Jacket; camel hair
Slacks; olive green flannel
Shirt; cream broadcloth
Tie; olive green and camel stripes

Sport Coat
Jacket; teal and camel heather tweed
Slacks; teal gabardine or camel flannel
Shirt; yellow tone-on-tone stripe
Tie; camel, blue and gold stripes

Sport Coat
Jacket; camel flannel
Slacks; brown, green and beige plaid
Shirt; beige broadcloth
Tie; forest green club

Sport Coat
Jacket; camel and brown herringbone
Slacks; chocolate or camel flannel
Shirt; cream, peach or yellow
Tie; brown, camel and cream stripes

Wardrobe Planning   7

PULL IT TOGETHER WITH COLOR

G etting your wardrobe together will be a fun and challenging experience if you approach it with the same degree of intelligence and preparation you would give to any project in which you will be investing thousands of dollars. Your immediate goal is to get this basic group of clothes together as quickly as possible. Your ultimate goal is to look your best at all times.

Examine the following Basic Wardrobe Plan chart. An effective wardrobe should have at least *one* item in each category. Your lifestyle will dictate in which areas you need more. For example: If you are a businessman who wears a suit to work every day, you would need a minimum of five suits. If, in your work environment, you can alternate with sport coats and slacks, you would need three suits. On the other hand, if you are in an occupation which never requires wearing a suit and you have a very casual personal life to boot, one marrying and burying suit might be enough.

Balance the wardrobe needs of your occupational and social lifestyles. We recognize that you probably already own many of the garments listed. Study the chart, however, as if you had absolutely nothing to wear and were starting from scratch to put together an ideal wardrobe. Considering each

garment you have, decide if you can check that item off your chart. Make decisions about questionable items which might need replacing or updating. On the pages following the wardrobe chart in this chapter, you will find additional information about each type of garment listed. If you have analyzed your lifestyle, you will know which type from each category fits your individual needs.

We have suggested a specific order for acquiring your suits, to enable you to have a workable wardrobe with the fewest number of clothes possible.

Regardless of how much money and how much time you might have to devote to the project, you probably will need from two to five years to put together this kind of a wardrobe. Proximity to a metropolitan area boasting fine menswear stores, or the ability to afford the luxury of a personal tailor, could greatly reduce your time schedule. However, you still must keep searching, with discipline and devotion to your plan, to collect notable accessories—after all, they are the frosting on your cake, identifying you as a man possessing great personal style.

PULL IT TOGETHER WITH COLOR

BASIC WARDROBE PLAN CHART

Shoes (4 pairs)
- ☐ Dress—plain toe
- ☐ Business—textured upper
- ☐ Sport—leather moccasin toe
- ☐ Casual—your choice

Belts (3)
- ☐ Plain buckle, smooth leather
- ☐ Textured leather
- ☐ Your choice

Socks
- ☐ Dark neutrals (12 pairs)
- ☐ White athletic (6 pairs)

Ties (3 per suit)
- ☐ 1 Rep tie
- ☐ 1 Club tie
- ☐ 1 Ivy League or plain tie

Coats (2)
- ☐ Topcoat
- ☐ All-weather coat
- ☐ Car coat
- ☐ Short jacket

Suits (1-5)
- ☐ 1: Medium to dark neutral, plain or textured
- ☐ 2: Dark neutral, solid or pinstripe, plain or textured
- ☐ 3: Light to medium neutral or basic color, plain or textured
- ☐ 4: Your choice
- ☐ 5: Your choice

Formal Attire
- ☐ Tuxedo
- ☐ Shirt, studs, suspenders, tie, cummerbund
- ☐ Shoes-socks

Personal Wear
- ☐ Underwear
- ☐ Handkerchiefs—for pocket decorative accessory and nose care
- ☐ Bathrobe—terrycloth, velour or silk

- ☐ Caftan
- ☐ Slippers—leather, cloth; thongs, slippersox

Casual Wear (wash and wear as needed)
- ☐ Pants: Slacks, denims, Levis, fatigues
- ☐ Shirts: Tee, polo, Hawaiian, Mexican Wedding, Ivy League, Western

Special Activities
- ☐ Appropriate clothing for tennis, racquetball, golf, swimming, surfing, surf sailing, sailing, boating, skiing, hunting, hiking or fishing
- ☐ Grubbies—for yard and house chores

Sport Coats (1-3)
- ☐ 1: Blazer—plain, patterned or textured
- ☐ 2: Sporty—patches; Ultra-suede™; textured or patterned
- ☐ 3: Elegant—velveteen or cashmere

Slacks (2 per sport coat)
- ☐ 1: Solid color
- ☐ 2: Textured
- ☐ 3: Patterned

Dress Shirts (5 per suit)
- ☐ 1: Broadcloth, your white
- ☐ 2: Broadcloth, light color
- ☐ 3: Oxford, your white or light color
- ☐ 4: Tone-on-tone broadcloth, your white or light color
- ☐ 5: Stripe, windowpane or box plaid

Sport Shirts (2 or more)
- ☐ Woven: Oxford cloth—solid color, print, plaids, checks, stripes; button-down or standard collar; long or short sleeves

Sweaters (several)
- ☐ Cardigan or coat
- ☐ V-Neck—fine knit, bulky
- ☐ Crew—fine knit, textured or bulky
- ☐ Vest—sleeveless slip-over or button
- ☐ Turtleneck—thin cotton, heavy or bulky
- ☐ Mock turtleneck—fine knit, textured or bulky

COATS

Topcoat

This coat is essential only to those men living in colder climates. Depending on how much warmth you need, the lining of your topcoat may be removable. You will wear this coat for years, so you should choose a classic, plain style in a straight silhouette which will stay in fashion. You could buy plain or textured wool fabric, remembering that textured fabric shows wrinkles less. A medium-to-dark value in one of your neutral colors will go with all of your clothes and show soil less readily. The hem of this coat should be about one inch below your knee.

All-Weather Coat

An all-weather coat should be included in most men's wardrobes. Buy it in a water-proof poplin, gabardine or twill type fabric, preferably in a polyester/cotton blend. If your all-weather coat has a removable lining, it may double as a topcoat if you happen to travel in colder climates. The straight silhouette is most popular, wearable and timeless, but the belted trench coat would be a good choice for the tall or slim man. Choose a light to medium value in your grays or beiges. Wear your all-weather coat above the knee unless you are tall, then you may wear it just below.

TOPCOAT

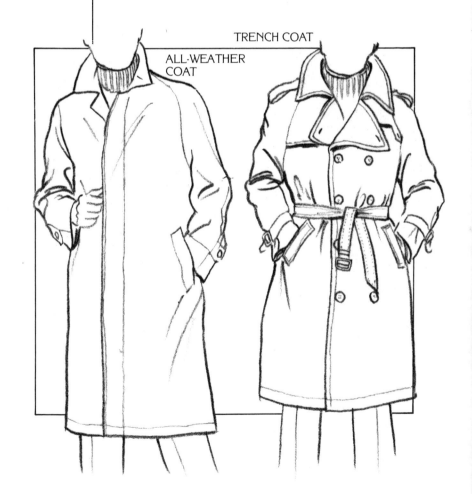

ALL-WEATHER COAT

TRENCH COAT

PULL IT TOGETHER WITH COLOR

Car Coat

Your choice of a car coat most definitely should be dictated by your lifestyle and personality. You may purchase only one of these in your lifetime, so let it reflect the real you and the way you live. This popular garment is also known as a stadium coat in its longer and dressier version. In shearling lamb, the car coat creates the elegant-casual, macho look of the *Marlboro Man*. In other fabrics, the lumber jacket, hunter's coat, field jacket or quilted coat fits the needs of the active outdoor man or the spectator of outdoor games. It is absolutely essential for the father of athletic sons and daughters who will spend years of his life standing on cold, wet, windy fields or sitting in chilly bleachers. Select your car coat in medium-to-dark values of your neutrals or basic colors. The fabric should be plain, textured, patterned, quilted or of leather, but it has got to be warm and durable. Your car coat should come a few inches below your crotch to cover your rump. When you sit down, unbutton your bottom button so your coat does not become rump-sprung or bulgy in the back.

STADIUM CAR COAT   STADIUM JACKET   SHEARLING

Short Jacket

Current titles for this ubiquitous coat include: Bomber, baseball, Eisenhower, windbreaker or "Members Only" jacket. You need at least one windbreaker of waterproof fabric in one of your bright or basic colors. Choose additional designs and fabrics in medium to dark values of your neutral or basic colors, as your lifestyle demands. Length can vary from waist to hipline. Shorter men should choose the shorter versions.

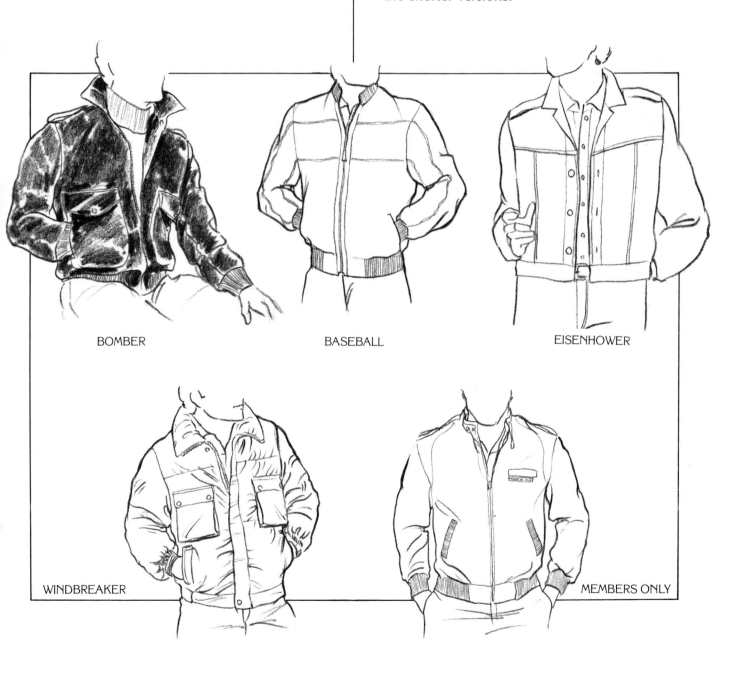

BOMBER

BASEBALL

EISENHOWER

WINDBREAKER

MEMBERS ONLY

PULL IT TOGETHER WITH COLOR

SUITS

We meet as many clients who have too many suits as we do men who have too few. By now you are aware that we encourage you to limit the number of your clothes to a bare minimum and think in terms of better quality garments and classic styling. By avoiding extremes in fabric and styling, classic clothes are not rendered obsolete by changing fashion. A good classic suit of worsted wool should give proud service for at least five years.

Every man needs at least *one* suit; most men need more. Depending on whether yours is a one-, three- or five-suit wardrobe, we recommend a specific order of acquisition. The color, texture and design of the fabric, along with the cut of the suit, determine whether it is all-purpose, dressy, business or casual.

Light-colored fabric shows soil, while very dark fabric shows lint and spots. Fabric of medium color forgives abuse more easily.

Smooth, plain fabric looks elegant, but it will show wrinkles more readily. Fabric with a woven texture or design shows wrinkles less and is more forgiving of spots and stains.

Dark, smooth, plain fabric is appropriate for most dress-up occasions in your social life. This type of suit fabric is also appropriate for those business occasions when you really want a power look — for meetings with your loan officer, presentations, speeches to your professional group, etc. Dark-colored fabric shows spots and lint most readily, so you always should consider where you are going before you put on a dark suit. If you are a neatnik there's no problem, but if you are a natural-born slob you'll save your dark suit for special occasions.

ONE-SUIT WARDROBE

The man who has only occasional need for a suit should buy a classic, 3-piece, vested style for long fashion life. If you're one of these men, choose a medium-to-dark neutral so that it will be more dressy. The fabric should be plain or slightly textured, or it could have an indistinct pattern. Buy worsted wool or a wool and polyester blend so the jacket, vest and pants will hold their shape. This suit should be the best quality you can afford because you probably will wear it only for important or ceremonial occasions—attending weddings, funerals and church services; patronizing good restaurants or theaters; and participating in business or social functions which require a suit, even for those with the most casual lifestyles.

Experience has shown that if we can once get a non-suit-wearing man into a quality garment, he really gets turned on to his new image. Predictions of the demise of traditional men's suit styles when the hippie generation reached maturity never materialized because once those kids got a taste of the gray flannel suit, they were hooked.

ABOUT YER SIGN...

122

THREE-SUIT WARDROBE

The three-suit wardrobe is for the man who doesn't need to wear a suit every day. He alternates suits with sport coats and slacks for his work or personal life. If you're one of these men, acquire your three suits with your immediate goal in mind, to get this basic group together quickly.

1. Your first purchase should be a three-piece, vested suit in a medium-to-dark neutral. The fabric may be textured or indistinctly patterned. This suit, appropriate for business or dress, will serve as the workhorse of your suit collection.

2. Your second acquisition should be a three-piece, vested suit in a neutral color of dark value and plain fabric. Your dress suit, this can double as your power look for business. If your physique and personality will allow, choose a more high-styled, shaped jacket.

3. Your third purchase will be a two- or three-piece suit, whichever you prefer, in a medium-to-light neutral color. You will want to vary the color of the fabric and the texture or pattern from Suit Number 1. This suit could be of a lighter weight fabric to enable your collection to function effectively year 'round. More casual than Suit Number 1, it would be appropriate for business and casual dress. You can extend the usefulness of this third suit if it is a style which looks good worn without a tie, with shirt collar unbuttoned or with a thin cotton turtleneck sweater.

PULL IT TOGETHER WITH COLOR

FIVE-SUIT WARDROBE

The man who wears a suit every day needs a minimum of five suits, so that he doesn't get too predictable. If you're one of these men, though, don't become addicted to suit collection. If you have too many, they'll lose their style before they are decently worn out. Instead, buy fewer and better. If you must collect something, old coins or vintage cars provide a more profitable investment.

1. Choose first a three-piece, vested suit in a medium-to-dark neutral fabric with texture or an indistinct pattern. If it is of worsted wool and the finest quality you can afford, it will be your power look for business and the backbone of your wardrobe.

2. Add a three-piece, vested suit of a dark neutral color in a plain fabric. This will be your dress suit for important business functions and your social life.

3. Your third acquisition should be a two-piece suit, basically the same style as Suit Number 1, but of a different neutral color and a different fabric. If the first suit is a textured fabric, then this one should be patterned for variety. This suit will give you another power look for business.

4. Next, add a two- or three-piece suit in a medium to light neutral color. This suit can be a more contemporary style and of a softer weave and texture, such as flannel. A lighter color will expand your wardrobe for summer, while you can also accessorize it for cooler weather with your sweater vest and your knit ties. If you enjoy sweater vests or novelty vests, make this a two-piece suit.

5. Finally, select a two- or three-piece suit, this one a medium-to-dark basic color or one of your neutrals. You might want to have this suit really reflect your personality with more design details or a more distinct pattern in the fabric. Such an approach will add spice to your wardrobe, and because you do not have to wear this suit every day, you will not tire of it.

FORMAL ATTIRE

"Formal wear lifts a man out of the ordinary, if he should be ordinary to begin with."

Roger Smith, 1832

There are two types of formal dress, and usually no question arises as to which you are to wear because most invitations indicate whether the occasion will be white tie or black tie.

White Tie

This means full evening dress: Tails, boiled shirt, high starched collar, white bow tie, patent leather shoes, nylon hose, high silk hat and gloves.

Black Tie

This refers to a dinner jacket or tuxedo and allows you some leeway. The classic tuxedo is made of smooth, plain, black fabric and has black satin lapels. With it, you will wear a black butterfly bow tie and a black cummerbund to match your lapels. Complete your white knife-pleated evening shirt with shirt studs and cuff links. Wear black or white suspenders, nylon hose and shoes with a smooth, plain toe of either black calf or black patent.

There are variations on the tuxedo theme which may keep the spice in your formal life — but simplicity is always the safest way to go.

1. A white dinner jacket is for resort or tropic wear and is always worn with black trousers.

2. If you attend fewer than three formal functions a year, you might be wiser to rent your formal clothes. Any first-rate formal wear rental store offers a generous selection of sizes and on-premise fitters. If you fit fairly well into ready-to-wear, you can expect a good fit in a rental tux. Rental of formal wear is a thriving business, and most men among the famous and mighty have rented a tux or tails at one time or another. Shop for the best quality and selection.

3. If your need for formal wear increases and you are thinking of buying your own, consider this approach. While shopping for your new tux, explore the possibility of buying a used tuxedo from your local rental store. Styles in tuxedos change slowly. Plan ahead if you decide to buy. If you have a large family of boys, you might consider purchasing a tux for the first prom. One of us fell heir to one which was worn by all of her sons, who ranged from 5-foot-6 to 6 feet tall. We haven't yet decided if it really was good fortune, having done the alterations for each kid and many of their friends. They are all grown and gone now, and we are considering casting the old tux in bronze.

4. Colored tuxedos are for spring and summer weddings and proms. The mature man will be more comfortable in black. If black is not your color, however, you might consider navy, gray, dark brown, dark maroon or deep forest green. The Southeast and Southwest are more relaxed about the color of formal wear. If you live east of the Mississippi or in a conservative community, however, go with black.

PULL IT TOGETHER WITH COLOR

5. As an alternative to the conventional tuxedo, you might consider wearing your dark dress suit or a velvet dinner jacket. The velvet dinner jacket may be worn with regular or matching velvet trousers. If your jacket has a pattern, wear it with black or blue evening trousers. Velvet jackets look very romantic with a silk ascot and an open-necked shirt. But be aware that local customs vary. If you are considering such an investment and you are uncertain about its propriety, talk to the manager of your local luxury menswear store before you buy anything.

SPORT COATS

You will need one to three sport coats, depending on your lifestyle.

Patterned jackets combine with plain slacks and vice versa. The visual balance of your chest and hips should help you decide whether your sport coats are plain or patterned. If your shoulders are large and your hips slim, pick a plain or indistinct pattern or textured fabric for the coat. Narrow shoulders benefit from a patterned or textured jacket because it adds to your apparent size. A balanced physique can go either way. You should be aware, however, that combinations of coats and slacks are made more easily when your jacket is a plain or textured fabric. A patterned jacket, on the other hand, almost always dictates plain slacks.

Here is the order in which you might purchase these:

1. Blazer style—plain or muted pattern as physique suggests, in a neutral color.

2. Very sporty—textured or patterned, patch pockets, patch elbows, top stitching or piping. Fabric could be wool, leather or Ultrasuede™ in any of your neutrals or basic colors.

3. Casual but elegant sports attire—soft wool, velveteen or cashmere.

PULL IT TOGETHER WITH COLOR

SLACKS

You will need a minimum of two pairs of slacks per sport coat. They can be plain or patterned, depending on the coat. If you choose a pattern, it should be scaled to your size and personality. Plan to have some of your slacks of wool, some combinations of wool and polyester and others of 100% polyester that looks like wool.

DRESS SHIRTS

You need five dress shirts per suit. The most attractive and comfortable fabrics will be 100% cotton or a cotton-poly blend. Broadcloth and batiste both are fine smooth weaves, but batiste is more sheer. You will, of course, choose your own shade of white. These shirts will coordinate with your other suits and sport coats.

Choose:
—1 white broadcloth or batiste
—1 light-color broadcloth or batiste
—1 white or light-colored Oxford cloth
—1 white or light tone-on-tone broadcloth or batiste
—1 broadcloth in a pattern—striped, window-pane, box plaid. Use two or three colors only. This shirt is optional: if you prefer, you may repeat one of the first four choices.

TIES

You need three ties per suit: see chapter 3, page 69. 1 rep tie; 1 club tie; and 1 Ivy League or plain tie. These ties should harmonize with your suits and be scaled to your size.

Choose silk ties or quality polyester ties which look and feel like silk. Bulky ties form a poor knot.

SPORT SHIRTS

Choose long or short sleeves, depending on the climate, and go with woven cotton or a cotton-polyester blend. You should have two to four sport shirts, which can be worn with slacks, sweaters, or sport coats. They may be solids or prints, checks or stripes, with a button-down or a standard collar. The colored Oxford cloth button-down shirts are a good choice.

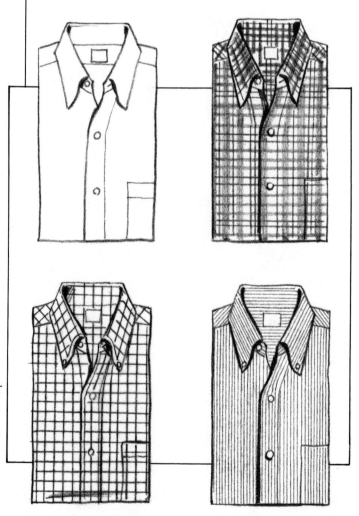

SWEATERS

Sweaters are available in a wide choice of styles and fabrics, adding variety and dimension to your total look. Your personality and your lifestyle determine quantity and style. Here are some of your options:

Cardigan — Button front, fine knit or bulky. Could have a tie belt.

V-neck — Pullover, fine knit or bulky.

Crew neck — Pullover, fine knit, textured or bulky.

Vest — Sleeveless pullover or button front, fine or bulky knit.

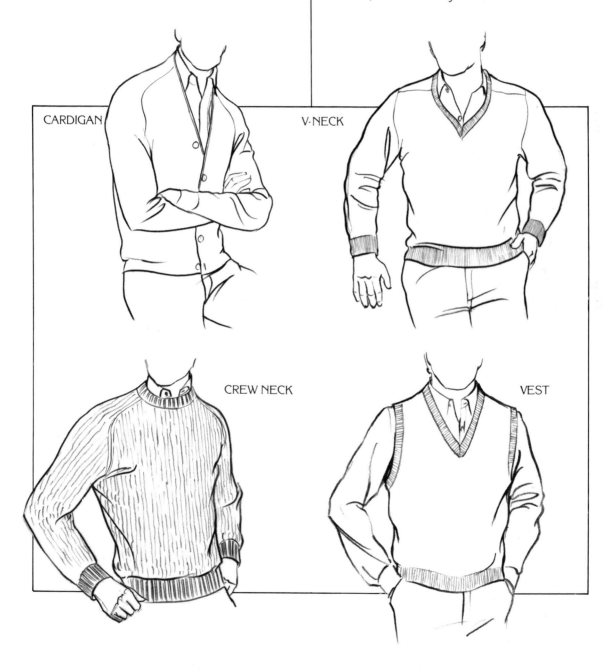

CARDIGAN V-NECK

CREW NECK VEST

PULL IT TOGETHER WITH COLOR

Turtleneck — Pullover, thin cotton or wool, heavy or bulky. Most men look dashing in turtlenecks. Try thin cotton and then add others as your neck and personality will allow.

Mock turtleneck — Pullover, fine knit, textured or bulky. Moderately high neck which hugs the throat. The mock turtle is becoming on most body types.

Sweater sleeves come in a variety of styles: Inset, saddle, raglan and drop sleeves. The inset and the saddle sleeve styles are becoming on all body types. Drop shoulder and raglan sleeved styles, on the other hand, demand well proportioned, tapered shoulders.

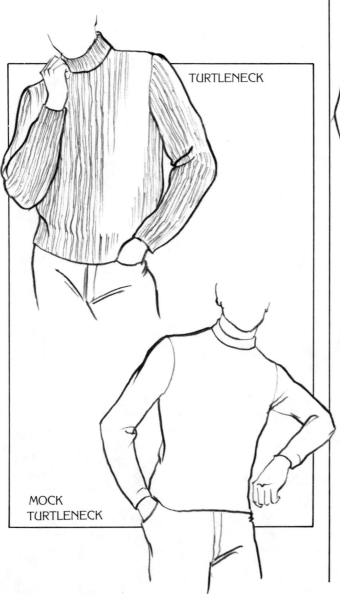

TURTLENECK

MOCK TURTLENECK

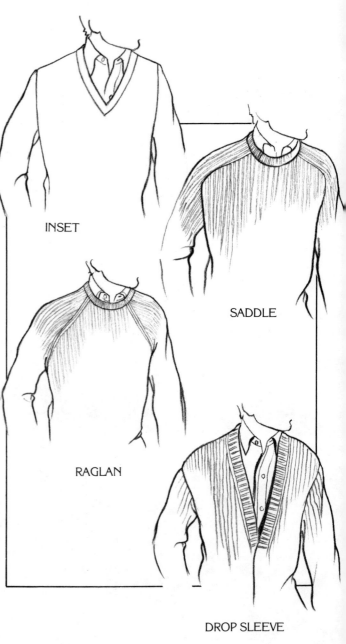

INSET

SADDLE

RAGLAN

DROP SLEEVE

CASUAL WEAR

"Casual" refers to the situations in which you'll be wearing these clothes, but it also signifies their ease of care: Wash and wear. Pants may include cotton-polyester slacks, denims, Levis, and fatigues.

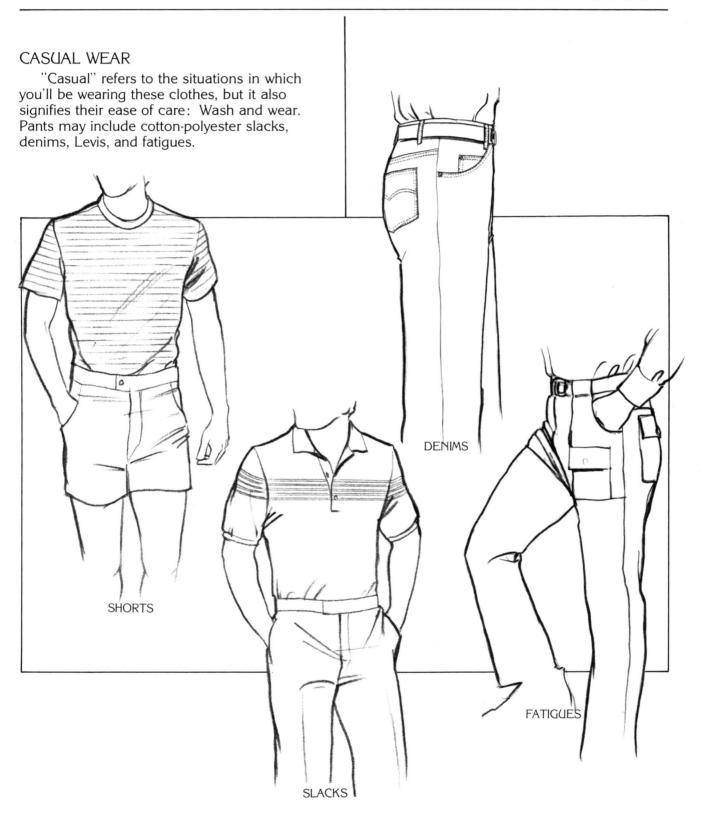

DENIMS

SHORTS

FATIGUES

SLACKS

PUT IT TOGETHER WITH COLOR

Shirts may be cotton or cotton-polyester with long or short sleeves in a plain or printed fabric. Styles include T-shirts, polo, Hawaiian, Mexican wedding, Ivy League and Western shirts.

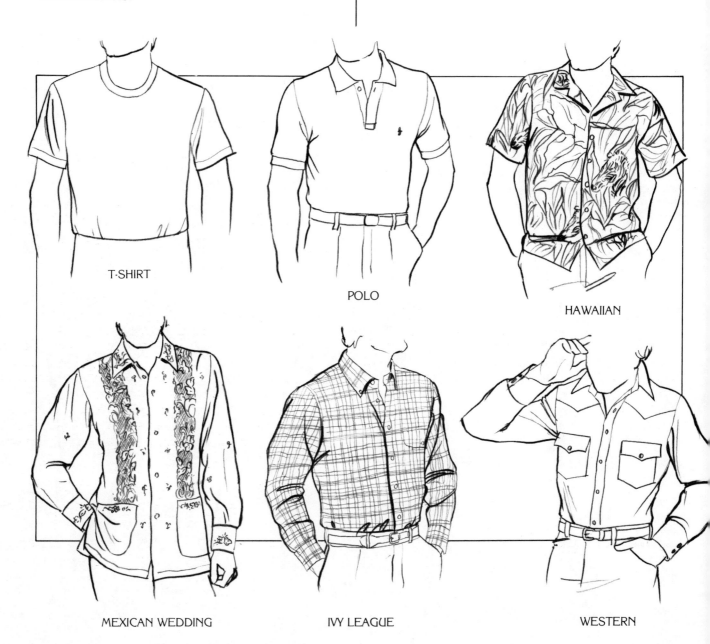

T-SHIRT

POLO

HAWAIIAN

MEXICAN WEDDING

IVY LEAGUE

WESTERN

SPECIAL ACTIVITIES

You need a warm-up or jogging suit in one of your best colors. It can be worn for some of your sports activities and around the house on weekends and evenings for comfort. A jogging outfit has become the supermarket status symbol. In addition, make sure you have the proper attire for the sport(s) you enjoy. Remember, you can have it together with a coordinated look even while playing tennis, racquetball or golf, or while swimming, surfing, sailing, boating, skiing, hunting, hiking, fishing, etc.

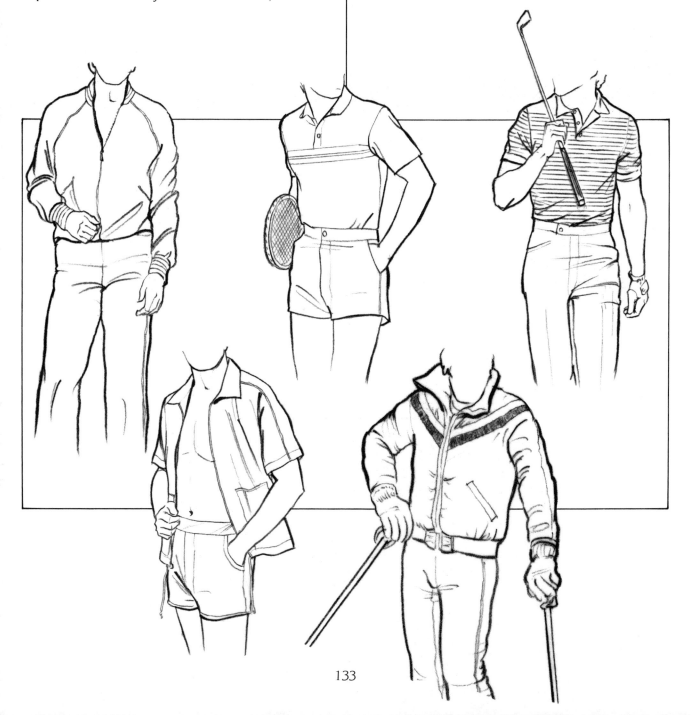

PUT IT TOGETHER WITH COLOR

Keep your grubbies for yard work and around the house. Even there, though think coordinates —wearing the right color T-shirt with your old pants as you mow the lawn Saturday mornings can make you the neighborhood celebrity.

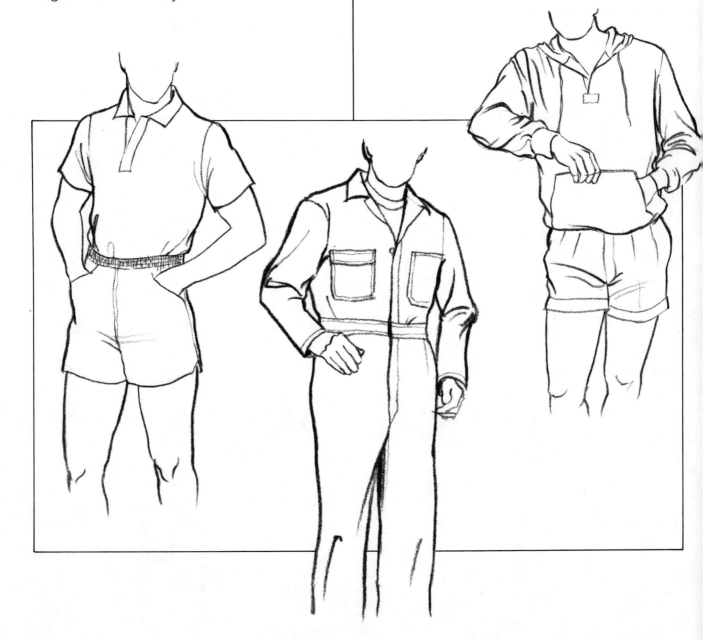

UNDERWEAR

Eight to ten T-shirts and shorts, depending on your laundry situation, should give you an ample supply.

SOCKS

Have at least a dozen pairs of socks for dress in only one or two of your darker neutral colors. Any other colors are considered extra. See chapter 8, page 151.

In addition, have six pairs of white athletic socks if you wear tennis or jogging shoes.

SLIPPERS

Leather or fabric house shoes, thongs or slipper socks all offer comfortable around-the-house footwear.

BATHROBE

Choose a bathrobe of terrycloth, velour or silk. Some men enjoy wearing a caftan to relax in.

HANDKERCHIEFS

You should have:

—1 dozen handkerchiefs for personal use, always chalk white.

—2 pocket squares for business suit pockets. Try to pick up a color from your tie, but don't attempt to match its print or pattern. See chapter 8, page 152.

SHOES

Appropriate shoe styles provide a vital element in your total look. See chapter 8, pages 146-150.

You need:

—1 pair dress shoes: Plain toe, smooth leather, thin sole, tie or slip-on.

—1 pair business dress shoes: Of the same color as your dress shoes, textured leather upper or wing tip, with more substantial sole.

—1 pair sporty leather shoes: Moccasin toe, tie or loafer.

—1 pair casual run-around shoes, your choice: Topsider, deck, tennis or jogging shoes.

PUT IT TOGETHER WITH COLOR

WINTER - An Example of a Basic Wardrobe Plan

SUITS		SHIRTS	TIES
For Business: 3 pc. Medium to dark gray or blue-gray Plain or textured Worsted wool		2 - White broadcloth 1 - White or blue oxford, button-down 1 - Light blue 1 - White with blue or gray pinstripe	1 - Solid, dark blue silk 1 - Rep silk blue-gray-white or blue-white-maroon 1 - Club silk, blue with red or white
For Dress: 3 pc. Dark navy Solid or prinstiped Plain or textured Worsted wool		1 - White batiste or broadcloth 1 - White tone-on-tone 1 - Iced blue 1 - Iced pink 1 - Pale gray with white collar and cuffs or your choice	1 - Solid silk maroon 1 - Navy with white or maroon, small dots on silk 1 - Red-white-navy rep stripe silk
For Business or Casual: 2 pc. Light to medium blue, gray or charcoal Plain or textured Wool or wool-poly blend		1 - White oxford, button-down 1 - Red and white candy stripe 1 - White and blue or gray pinstripe or box check 2 - Your choice	1 - Solid red, blue or black knit or club 1 - Black-white-red rep or geometric silk 1 - Club black or navy with white, red or maroon motif

SPORT COATS	PANTS		
Navy blue blazer Silver antique buttons	1 - Lt. to med. gray flannel or worsted 1 - Solid taupe or navy-white-maroon stripe, check or plaid. Scale to your size	1 - Blue, pink or yellow oxford, button-down 1 - Plain or stripe polo or your choice	1 - Navy, red or gray wool knit 2 - Ivy League navy with red or white motif
Gray Herringbone or tweed wool (patch elbows) or Black or navy Leather or Ultrasuede™	1 - Black or navy 1 - Maroon	1 - White, red, navy or black mock or turtleneck 1 - Your choice	Use ties from above
Maroon blazer velveteen or wool	1 - Gray from above 1 - Black garbadine	1 - Ice pink open neck 1 - White batiste or silk	1 - Club black with maroon motif 1 - Maroon silk print ascot in open neck collar opt.
	Dark blue denim Gray brushed cotton or corduroy Taupe or navy cotton-poly wash-n-wear	Blue print long sleeves cotton-poly Blue-white-red or pink polo	

WINTER - An Example of a Basic Wardrobe Plan

JEWELRY	BELTS	SHOES	SOCKS	SWEATERS	JACKETS/COATS
Silver collar pin	Black calf smooth Silver buckle	Black Oxford or slip-ons Smooth toe	Black or navy Calf or knee high		Gray or taupe Raincoat
1 set of silver cuff links	Same as above	Black plain or cap toe Oxford	Black or navy		
	Black or cordovan textured (lizard) Silver buckle	Black wing tip	Black or navy	Gray, navy or maroon V-neck vest pullover lambswool or cashmere	
	Black or cordovan smooth or textured	Black or cordovan slip-on with tassel or moccasin toe	Navy, gray or maroon	Gray, navy or maroon V-neck long-sleeve pull-over wool or cashmere	
	Red-navy or black webbing	Black or cordovan loafers or short boots	Black, navy	Red, gray, navy or black cardigan	
Silver neck chain (opt.)	Black calf leather	Same as one above	Black		
	Tooled leather or one of the above	Black or cordovan penny loafers Topsiders, deck, or jogging	Navy White		Navy, black, or maroon Windbreaker

PUT IT TOGETHER WITH COLOR

SUMMER - An Example of a Basic Wardrobe Plan

SUITS		SHIRTS	TIES
For Business: 3 pc. Blue-gray Herringbone, stripe or glen plaid Worsted wool		2 - Off-white broadcloth 1 - Powder blue 1 - Stripe blue 1 - Off-white or blue oxford, button-down	1 - Blue-gray-wine rep stripe 1 - Navy club with maroon lt. blue motif 1 - Blue solid silk
For Dress: 3 pc. French navy Solid or stripe		1 - Off-white tone-on-tone 1 - Off-white batiste 2 - Light blue or aqua 1 - Lt. pink	1 - Burgundy solid silk 1 - Navy blue with white, lt. blue or maroon dot silk 1 - Navy-burgundy rep
For Business or Casual: 2 pc. Cadet blue Heathered wool flannel		1 - Blue oxford, button-down 1 - Off-white oxford, button-down 1 - Off-white and blue window pane 1 - Lt. mauve oxford	1 - Blue knit 1 - Multi-color 1 - Blue-maroon-white rep

SPORT COATS	PANTS		
Burgundy plain, herringbone or muted plaid blazer blazer	1 - Burgundy 1 - Rose beige	1 - Rose beige broadcloth 1 - White-burgundy stripe oxford, button- down 1 - One of the above or your choice	1 - Burgundy knit 1 - Coordinated rep or club
French Navy or cadet blue blazer	1 - Blue-gray flannel 1 - Coordinated muted pattern	1 - Use one of the above: pink, mauve, blue or off-white 1 - Your choice	1 - Blue or burgundy knit 1 - Navy and wine rep (see above)
Burgundy Ultra- suede™	1 - Gray or navy 1 - Navy-burgundy sm. check or stripe	1 - Pink or mauve batiste or silk 1 - Your choice	Same as above
	1 - Blue brushed denim 1 - Navy cotton-poly wash-n-wear	1 - Blue or burgundy print long sleeves, cotton-poly 1 - Blue, pink, mauve or burgundy polo	

SUMMER - An Example of a Basic Wardrobe Plan

JEWELRY	BELTS	SHOES	SOCKS	SWEATERS	JACKETS/COATS
Silver collar pin	Black calf smooth Silver buckle	Black Oxford Smooth toe	Black or navy	Gray vest	Gray or beige raincoat
Silver cuff links	Same as above	Black oxford Plain or cap toe	Black		
	Black or cordovan Smooth or textured (lizard) Silver buckle	Black or cordovan slip-on or wing-tip Oxford	Black or navy		
	Same as above	Burgundy loafer	Burgundy	Burgundy V-neck pull-over, cashmere	
	Black or cordovan	Black or cordovan slip-on or Oxford wing-tip (from above)	Black	Lt. blue, navy, or gray V-neck, long-sleeved pullover	
Silver neck chain (opt.)	Burgundy smooth	Burgundy Oxford or slip-on (from above)	Burgundy		
	Blue-wine webbing	Cordovan loafer or topsider or navy deck	Burgundy White	Med. blue cardigan lambswool or cashmere	Burgundy or cadet blue windbreaker

PUT IT TOGETHER WITH COLOR

SPRING - An Example of a Basic Wardrobe Plan

SUITS		SHIRTS	TIES
For Business:		1 - Lt. Cream	1 - Clear navy solid
3 pc. Med. Blue w/tan thread		1 - Blue broadcloth	1 - Blue-tan-cream-rep
Herringbone, stripe or soft plaid		1 - Blue oxford, button-down	1 - Blue club with off-white, peach or
Worsted wool		1 - Lt. peach broadcloth	red motif
		1 - Lt. beige	
For Dress:		1 - Off-white tone-on-tone	1 - Navy and red club
3 pc. Clear navy		1 - Lt. cream	1 - Navy and lt. blue rep
Plain		1 - Lt. blue batiste	1 - Navy, cream or red sm. dot
Worsted wool		1 - Lt. peach batiste	
		1 - Lt. gray batiste	
For Business or Casual:		1 - Cream and brown pin-stripe	1 - Brown and cream rep
2 pc. Milk chocolate brown		1 - Lt. periwinkle blue	1 - Brown and periwinkle rep stripe
Plain or textured		1 - Beige and peach stripe or window	1 - Brown-gold-peach plaid or paisley
Wool		pane	
		2 - Cream oxford, button-down	

SPORT COATS	PANTS		
Camel hair blazer	1 - Milk chocolate brown	1 - Lt. gold oxford, button-down	1 - Brown-tan-navy rep
	1 - Clear navy	1 - Lt. periwinkle oxford, button-down	1 - Solid knit in chocolate, navy red
		2 - Polo, gold, peach or red	or maize
		1 - Cream-tan-navy, cotton-poly, plaid, check or stripe	
Navy blazer	1 - Lt. dove gray flannel	1 - Lt. blue and navy print	1 - Navy-tan-gray rep
Gold buttons	1 - Tan gabardine	Several - Polo, cream, lime green, peach, red, aqua, blue or maize	
Tan or milk chocolate brown leather	Use any of the above of your choice	1 - Brown plaid	Open collars
		1 - Casual of your choice	
	1 - Blue denim	1 - Blue-tan and cream plaid or check	
	1 - Tan cotton-poly, wash-n-wear	Western style opt.	
		2 - Your choice	

SPRING - An Example of a Basic Wardrobe Plan

JEWELRY	BELTS	SHOES	SOCKS	SWEATERS	JACKETS/COATS
Gold tie bar	Black calf smooth Gold buckle	Black Oxford or or slip-ons Smooth toe	Black or navy		Tan Raincoat
Gold cuff links	Same as above	Black Oxford Plain or cap toe	Black or navy		
	Brown cowhide or lizard Gold buckle	Brown Oxford or slip-on	Brown	Tan or lt. gold V-neck vest, plain or argyle, lambs-wool or cashmere	
Gold neck chain (opt.)		Black, navy or tan loafers			
Same as above	Black or tan			1 - Navy or camel V-neck, long sleeved pullover, wool or cashmere	
	Chocolate or tan, smooth or textured	Chocolate or tan loafers or topsiders			
	1 - Brown tooled leather, interest-ing buckle 1 - Brown-tan-red or navy webbing	Brown boots Brown or navy loafers, top-siders or deck shoes	Brown, navy or or tan	Red, camel or blue cardigan	Tan or cream windbreaker

PUT IT TOGETHER WITH COLOR

AUTUMN - An Example of a Basic Wardrobe Plan

SUITS	SHIRTS	TIES
For Business: 3 pc. Med. brown coffee Plain herringbone, stripe or glen plaid Worsted wool	1 - Cream broadcloth 1 - Cream with tan stripe 1 - Beige 1 - Periwinkle blue oxford, button-down 1 - Lt. peach	1 - Brown with cream or red motif club 1 - Brown and blue rep stripe 1 - Brown-peach, cream and blue rep stripe
For Dress: 3 pc. Dark brown Solid or herringbone stripe Worsted wool	1 - Cream batiste 1 - Ivory tone-on-tone 1 - Ivory with brown stripe 1 - Ivory with periwinkle blue stripe 1 - Ivory or Peach	1 - Solid brown silk 1 - Brown with cream dots club 1 - Brown with cream, red, gold or blue rep
For Business or Casual: 2 pc. Tan Solid Wool flannel or herringbone	1 - Ivory oxford, button-down 1 - Cream with gold stripe 1 - Beige with gold or blue box check 1 - Peach oxford, button-down 1 - Blue with tan stripe	1 - Solid brown knit 1 - Camel, brown, cream and blue stripe rep 1 - Tan knit or club

SPORT COATS	PANTS		
Camel blazer	1 - Chocolate brown 1 - Camel-brown check or plaid	1 - Lt. gold oxford, button-down 1 - Earth-tone plaid or check, long sleeves 1 - Peach, red or rust polo	1 - Gold knit 1 - Earth-tone paisley
Camel or rust herringbone, tweed or plaid	1 - Tan 1 - Rust brown	1 - Cream polo 1 - Your choice	1 - Rust brown knit
Brown leather	1 - Wear any of the above 1 - Your choice	1 - Peach polo 1 - Brown plaid or check Western	1 - Paisley silk ascot
	1 - Tan cotton-poly, wash-n-wear 1 - Blue periwinkle denim	1 - Polo, red, yellow, green, tan, etc. 1 - Your choice	

AUTUMN - An Example of a Basic Wardrobe Plan

JEWELRY	BELTS	SHOES	SOCKS	SWEATERS	JACKETS/COATS
Gold collar bar	Brown calf Gold buckle	Brown Oxford slip-on or Wing tip	Brown		Tan raincoat
Gold cuff links	Same as above	Chocolate brown or slip-on Plain or cap toe	Chocolate		
	Brown lizard Carmel smooth	Brown slip-on Camel slip-on	Brown Camel	Brown, camel, cream argyle, V-neck, slip- over vest	
		Brown loafers	Same as above	Gold crew-neck, slip-over, lambs- wool or cashmere	
		Rust brown slip-on or wing-tip Oxford	Rust brown Camel	Rust, camel or chocolate slip- over, cashmere	
			Brown		
	Brown tooled leather or striped webbing	Tan loafers topsiders or deck	Same as above	Camel or chocolate cardigan	Tan windbreaker

Collecting your clothes will be a satisfying experience if you stick to your plan, coordinate your colors and exercise discipline. While you are shopping for clothes, however, be alert to the accessories you see because that's the next topic we'll tackle.

Accessories

8

FINISH WITH FLAIR

The choice of accessories is a matter of taste. Good taste is the ability to recognize and enjoy what is handsome and excellent, a sense of what is harmonious, appropriate and socially proper. Some men are born with this sense, while others have to acquire it. Many things influence what is considered taste — where you live, your cultural environment, your age and your lifestyle. What is appropriate in Southern California, for example, is not necessarily proper in Washington, D.C.

Accessories, consisting of everything except your garments themselves, play an important part in any wardrobe. They may include shoes, belts, suspenders, gloves, hats, handkerchiefs, socks, jewelry, leather goods and sunglasses. It takes time, good planning and some imagination to accessorize your clothes properly and with flair. Choose accessories that harmonize with each other and that can be worn with more than one outfit. Select them for lasting value by investing the most money in timeless classics — quality leather, good metals and jewelry.

SHOES

Shoes reflect your taste as well as your clothes and tell much about the man wearing them. A man who buys fine leather shoes and then takes care of them shows he respects quality. In putting together a good wardrobe, shoes present a challenge because of the difficulty in obtaining good style, good fit and good color combined in the same shoe. Your shoes can make or break your total fashion look. They must harmonize in feeling with the clothes you are wearing.

Shoe colors for your season are listed on the chart *Basic Neutrals for Shoes*. Acceptable colors worldwide for business or dress shoes are black, brown and cordovan or burgundy. In buying shoes for casual wear, recognize that the shoes should be the same color as, or darker than, the pant leg. The eye will always go to the lightest part of the costume. Light colored shoes—white or bone—should be worn only with pants of the same or lighter value. The less contrast the better. If you choose colored shoes instead of neutral ones, they should match, blend or harmonize with the total costume.

FINISH WITH FLAIR

BASIC NEUTRALS FOR SHOES

Winter

☐ Black (essential)

☐ Cordovan or burgundy (optional)

☐ Navy (optional)

☐ Gray (optional)

☐ White (summer optional)

☐ Gray-bone taupe (summer optional)

Spring

☐ Black (essential)

☐ Medium brown (essential)

☐ Tan (essential)

☐ Navy (optional)

☐ Gray (optional)

☐ Yellow bone (summer optional)

Summer

☐ Black (essential)

☐ Cordovan or burgundy (essential)

☐ Navy (optional)

☐ Gray (optional)

☐ Off-white (summer optional)

Autumn

☐ Dark brown (essential)

☐ Rust brown (essential)

☐ Tan (essential)

☐ Medium brown (optional)

☐ Olive (optional)

☐ Yellow bone (summer optional)

FINISH WITH FLAIR

Your choice in men's shoe styles for business or dress fall into these general categories:

Type: Tie or slip-ons
Toe: Plain, moccasin or wing tip
Sole: Thin or thick, leather or rubber

You will find every imaginable combination of these three parts. The choice is less bewildering if you understand that a shoe with a plain, smooth upper and a thin leather sole is dressier than a sturdy, perforated or textured upper with a thick sole. Rubber soles are always casual. A shoe with moderate design detail or texture on the upper and a medium thick leather sole can be worn for both business dress with suits and for casual wear with slacks and a sport shirt. Very plain, smooth shoes with thin soles, on the other hand, look best with suits, dress slacks or formal attire. Textured moccasin toes and thick rubber soles are limited to casual attire.

HOW TO BUY SHOES

Shop for shoes in the mid-afternoon for a more realistic fit — by then your feet have spread as much as they are going to during the course of a day. Good shoes may be a pleasure to own, but a high price is no guarantee of good fit. When you shop, wear the same thickness of sock as you expect to wear with the shoes you're looking for. If you are shopping for dress shoes, don't wear tennis shoes into the store because any leather shoes will feel tight after you've been in canvas shoes.

Insist that the salesperson measure your foot each time you purchase a pair of shoes. The ball of your foot should rest at the shoe's greatest width. Then about half an inch of comfort space, depending on your foot size, should remain between the end of your big toe and the end of the shoe. The shoe's arch should be snug against your foot's arch, otherwise your foot must come down to meet the shoe at each step, creating discomfort and poor support. A shoe should bend just past the joint of your big toe. If it breaks farther toward the toe, then the shoe is either too long or else not proportioned to your foot—and in either case, blisters will result.

When a warm foot is slipped into a new shoe, it immediately feels comfortable because the shoe is cool. But don't let that sensation fool you. Your foot should settle into the shoe before its fit is determined. If the fit seems good, then you should purchase the shoes, but plan to wear them on soft carpet around your home, or slip-covered with old gym socks, for a few hours before making a final decision. That way, if the shoes are not right, you can then return them in "brand new" condition.

Wear new shoes at intervals until they are completely broken in. Each shoemaker has his own unique last, that is, a sizing proportion according to which he makes his shoes. If you should find one that fits perfectly, stick with that label! The maker has your foot in mind.

HOW TO CARE FOR YOUR SHOES

Polish new shoes before the first wearing with a neutral polish to retain the original color. They will be easier to shine each time, and they won't scuff as easily. After scuffs or nicks appear, a wax of the same color may be used. Keep your shoes clean and polished at all times.

Slip your feet into your footwear with a shoehorn. Allow leather shoes to air-dry for 24 hours between wearings. Have a pair of shoe trees for every pair of leather shoes you own, because when leather shoes get wet or are left unworn for a long time, shoe trees will maintain their shape. Wooden trees are best.

Keep your heels in good repair. If they are allowed to run down too far, it affects the balance and shape of the shoes. Rubber heals wear longer than leather.

Comfortable, handsome shoes of good quality are definitely worth having resoled if the work is done at the first sign of a wear-

through. Note, however, that if you wear them too thin, the sizing might be affected. Find a good shoemaker and let him extend the life of your faithful treasures.

If foot odor happens to be one of your problems, by all means make use of one of the many remedies available at your drugstore or from a podiatrist.

SHOE STYLES FOR THE COLLECTOR

Our survey revealed that most men have as many as 20 pairs of shoes apiece in their closets, possibly because they never throw a pair away. Sport and casual shoes are continually revolving fads. Nevertheless, if you are a shoe-aholic, you need to recognize that the eternal casuals and classics which the collector could safely acquire might include some of these:

Tennis Or Canvas

This type of shoe includes dozens of styles for as many activities. A canvas shoe of any style is very casual.

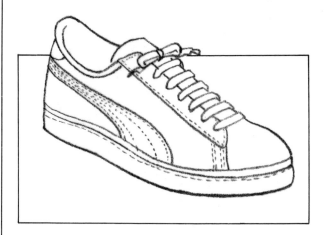

Topsiders

These usually have leather uppers with moccasin toes and rubber soles. Originally for boaters, they offer great comfort and go well with casual slacks, pants or Levis. When topsiders are new they look sharp, but they are hard to keep clean and by the time they've adjusted exquisitely to your feet, they are too dirty for clean company.

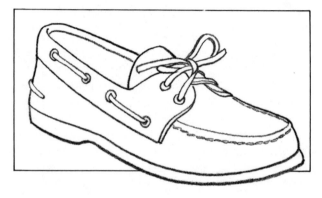

Moccasins

When copied from the original American Indian design, moccasins are the next best thing to going barefoot. Very casual, they make marvelous house shoes, especially when lined with fleece.

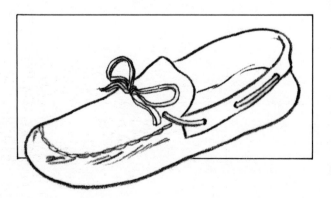

Running Shoes

These vary in style depending on the type of running you plan to do. Don't try to have them double as casual shoes, however, because they look odd with anything other than running clothes.

Sandals Or Thongs

These are basically beach and resort wear. In more relaxed sections of the country, sandals might creep into your casual attire, but keep your thongs for beach or pool.

Cowboy Boots

Originally worn with Levis and a horse, cowboy boots are still acceptable for casual or business dress in cow country. In other areas of the world, wear them on your own time with casual attire.

Canvas Or Leather Dance Shoes

Originally called jazz shoes, dance shoes feature clean lines and a rather nonchalant look which has been adapted for street wear. They are casual and look good with slacks and dressy sport clothes.

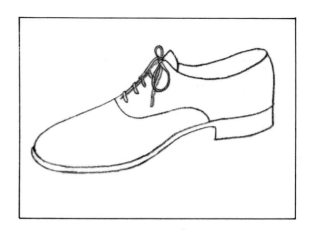

Dress Boots

These can be magnificent and expensive. Follow the same general rules as with dress shoes.

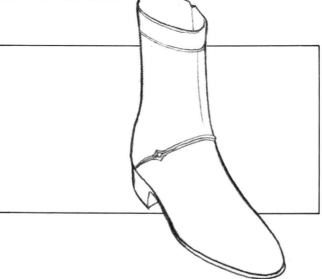

FINISH WITH FLAIR

Brogues, Chukka Boots, Loafers,
Hiking Boots, Clogs . . . Ad Infinitum
   Suit your footwear to your activity, but do
not try to have these collectibles do double
duty as your dress or business shoes.

BROGUES

LOAFERS

CHUKKA BOOTS

HIKING BOOTS

CLOGS

SOCKS

When you are wearing a suit or slacks, no one should be able to see your socks when you are standing, nor view your bare legs when you sit down.

The easiest approach to putting together a wardrobe of socks for business or dress is to:

—Have your socks the same color or value as your pants.

—Have your socks the same color as your shoes.

You may have a dozen pairs of the same color, some in a smooth knit, some ribbed, with regular or elastic tops.

If your socks refuse to stay up over full calves or thin legs, then you should wear garters. The alternative is calf-length socks, which most men abhor.

Patterned socks are for daytime and are best worn with plain suits or casual attire. Of heavier knits, they can be in bold, colorful designs. Casual socks are worn with tweeds and sport clothes.

Wear white socks with tennis shoes and most athletic foot-gear. And please, don't wear colored socks with athletic shoes!

If your feet perspire—especially in athletic socks—buy socks with cotton feet.

BELTS

Your belts form an important part of your wardrobe. For dress or business wear, choose smooth leather and a relatively small buckle of simple design. For sports, choose textured, worked or tooled leather and an ornate buckle to express your personality. Choose leather to match your shoes, and select the metal of the buckle according to your season.

Leathers used for belts are calfskin, cowhide, alligator, pigskin, ostrich, snakeskin and walrus. A tooled leather belt can be a prized possession. Buckles are made of every imaginable material and can become collector's items.

From 1 to 1-1/2 inches is a good basic belt width for most trousers. Any wider and the belt won't fit the belt loops of slacks; then it becomes more suitable to wear with Levis.

Fabric belts should be cleaned frequently. Leather belts can be wiped with a clean damp cloth and then carefully buffed with a soft dry cloth. Leather belts benefit from an occasional cleaning with saddle soap and a waxing to keep them supple. When not being worn, belts should be hung by their buckles on a hook.

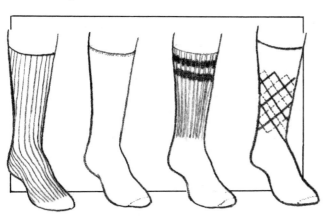

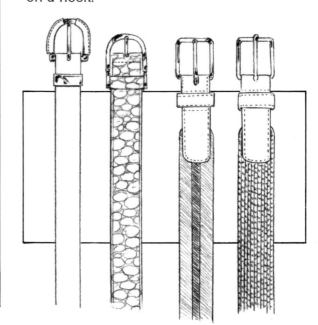

FINISH WITH FLAIR

HANDKERCHIEFS

A handkerchief in the breast pocket can perk up an otherwise somber outfit or help to balance the colors of your tie and shirt. You can match your handkerchief to your shirt color or to your tie color—matching a color from the tie is better—but regardless of which you choose, the handkerchief should not be of the same fabric or pattern. When in doubt, use white — a white handkerchief always gives a dressy look.

There are three ways to fold a handkerchief:

A handkerchief carried for you to use should be neatly folded and carried preferably in your front pants pocket or in a hip pocket, providing you have eliminated the fat wallet.

Neatly folded, extending about 3/4 inch out of the pocket.

With center and two corners extending out of the pocket. This style works well to show off a patterned handkerchief.

With three or four points extending about one inch out of the pocket. This style is good for hand-rolled hems.

LEATHER GOODS

Your watchband, wallet, billfold, coin or change purse, key case, briefcase, attache case, shoulder bag, wrist bag and/or notebook should coordinate in one of your darker neutrals for a put-together look.

Your travel case, shaving kit and suitcase could be of the same color or of coordinated colors.

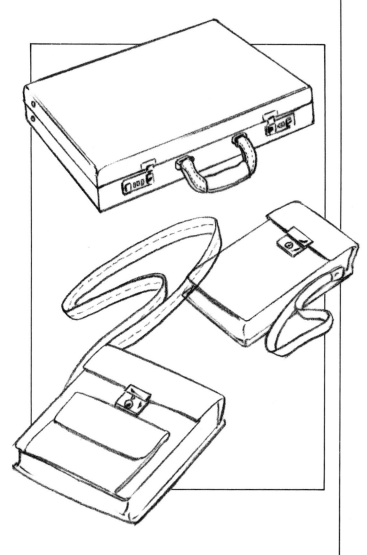

SUSPENDERS

Wear suspenders under vests or suit jackets for dress or business. They allow your trousers to fit more loosely at the waist, hang more smoothly and remain properly in place. Suspenders are especially useful for the portly man, the very active man and the very thin man.

Suspenders are essential with a tuxedo for evening dress, especially when you plan to dance.

HATS

While not as essential for the well-dressed man as they once were, hats are still worn in colder climates. Hats are intended to keep the head warm and dry, or to protect it from the sun. Choose hats to fit your personality and lifestyle, and be sure to wear one when you are exposed to the sun for an extended period of time—for tennis, boating, beach wear or spectator sports.

GLOVES

Gloves were initially worn to protect and warm the hands and to keep them clean. Because automobiles are cleaner and less frisky than horses, your need for gloves depends on your lifestyle and your part of the country. Fleece-lined leather gloves can be an important accessory if you live or work in a cold climate.

Men's gloves should be simple in style, whether they are worn for business or for

FINISH WITH FLAIR

sportswear. Choose sturdy leather in your medium to dark neutral colors. Elegant leather driving gloves add pizzazz to any man's image.

When wearing formal clothes or taking part in a wedding party, take the advice of a clothier in your area about the propriety of dress gloves.

SCARVES

Scarves are made of silk or wool. They can be worn as an ascot or draped, untied, around the neck or collar of a jacket or coat. In cold weather, the wool scarf provides marvelous warmth. The silk scarf is dressier, adding sophisticated flair.

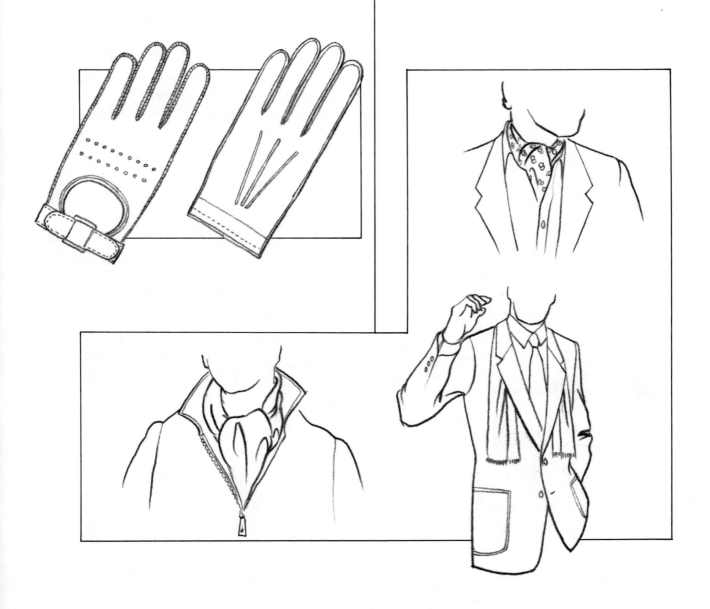

JEWELRY

The metal of your season will harmonize with your skin tone and go better with the colors you wear. Winters and Summers wear silver, platinum or white gold. Springs and Autumns wear yellow gold.

Brushed metal is the most dressy, especially if it is used with stones or pearls. Shiny metal is better for sporty or casual wear. If shiny and brushed metal are combined, the look will be less dressy. Metal watchbands are dressier, leather ones more casual.

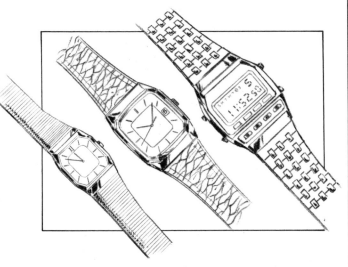

Keep your tie clasp, collar pin, cuff links, studs, neck chains, wrist chains and watches scaled to your size.

You need only one good pair of cuff links. The most elegant ones have matching sides connected by a chain or link. Flat gold or silver—copies of ordinary buttons—that may be plain or bear an initial engraved on both sides are very smart looking.

Collar pins are in when narrow ties are in and out when wide ties are in. If you like collar pins, get one in the metal of your season.

Before adding anything to your suit, shirt or tie for the world of business, consider your occupation and the people with whom you will be dealing. The more conservative types might be put off by any flashy display. If you enjoy lots of jewelry, wear it on your own time.

You will want to carry a pen or pencil, money clip or key ring in your own metal. A good silver or gold pen or pencil spells class for the businessman.

UMBRELLAS

The young or adventurous may prefer to dash pell mell without an umbrella. To arrive at your office or appointment with wet hair and water spots on your $500 suit, however, seems foolhardy. Choose a simple man's umbrella in a neutral color to coordinate with your all-weather coat.

Accessories are the condiments of your wardrobe. While you are making a careful collection, you also need to turn your attention to one of the most important purchases you'll ever make—your eyeglasses.

Eyewear 9

SEEING BETTER, LOOKING BEST

Eyeglasses are more than just another accessory — they are vital to your health and often to how effectively you deal with the world. Whether or not you wear glasses all the time, they are part of you and should complement your appearance and exemplify your personality and lifestyle.

Glasses today are such becoming fashion items that some people look better with than without them. Regardless of whether you look better with or without glasses, you should have more than one pair. When shopping for eyewear, take someone along who can be objective and helpful. Involved in your choices are:

Fashion — This refers to the eyeglasses themselves, the material of which they are constructed, the design and size of the frame, color of the lens, and shape of the ear piece. Be alert to changing fashion. You might need to change glasses to stay in style more frequently than you need to change your prescription.

Shape — The shape of the frame is determined by your facial contours and features. The rules of shape are general, modified according to each individual. To begin with, you need to be aware that different shapes of frames are available in different sizes. Then remember: The size of your face determines the size of the frame. Don't let your glasses wear you, which they will appear to do if the frames are too large. On the other hand, frames that are too small will cause your total image to lose impact.

Lifestyle — Classify your lifestyle and select eyewear accordingly. Are you a sophisticated, conservative, casual or high-fashion type? The latest Pierre Cardin frames might be smashing, but will they wear you? Delicate metal frames can be very flattering, but how will they survive your rough treatment? Are you an avant-garde artist wearing Daniel Webster frames?

If your health insurance offers an arrangement for cutrate eyewear, you should shop at several eyewear specialty stores to acquaint yourself with what is new and to establish your taste in current fashion. Then check to see if your outlet can supply the same glasses. This is really no time to economize. You need quality, but the appearance is equally important. Use the same care you would in shopping for a plastic surgeon. For some people, eyewear is a permanent facial detail.

Norman
These are good glasses for a round face. The upper frames match his hair. The lower frames are clear, giving a lift to the face and detracting from its fullness.

Reed
For a longer face, the entire frame and the temple were chosen in a color to match his hair. The colored frames break the length of his face.

Doug
An oval face can wear almost any shape of glasses. A man who does not want to call attention to his glasses, Doug chose a pair with unobtrusive wire frames on the upper and at the temples, and no frames on the lower.

Merrill
A small face benefits from frames which are clear on the bottom, top and the bridge, but which have a little color on the outer rims and temples. These glasses lighten and lengthen the center of his face and soften a long nose.

SUNGLASSES

If you wear glasses all the time, we discourage your trying to combine your regular glasses and sunshades into the same eyewear by using photo-sensitive lenses. Light-sensitive lenses often do not darken enough for strong sunlight outdoors, while they do not lighten enough inside, either. And the latter is important: People need to see your eyes if you are going to establish rapport.

Sunglasses are a fashion item. They should follow the same general rules that we've set out for other eyewear, but they can be fun, large and extreme—real macho! The lenses should harmonize with your eye color and the colors of your season.

Randy
Sunglasses can be large, extreme, high fashion and fun.

SEEING BETTER, LOOKING BEST

FRAMES

Frames should be as wide as the widest part of your face and in proportion to the shape and size of your face. Glasses should lift your face by having an upward line or curve on the upper frame. For good balance your eye should be in the center of the frame or lens. The lower frame should not repeat but complement your cheek and jawline. This means that you should not put round frames on a round face or square frames on a square face. The round face could wear a rounded square, and the square face a squared round.

Choose a high, slender or rounded bridge for a small nose; a low, thick or straight bridge is more becoming for a long nose.

Plastic frames should blend with your complexion and hair coloring. Winters wear charcoal-brown, gray-blues, or gray if they have gray hair. Summers look good in rose-browns, blue-grays, and gray with gray hair. Springs wear medium to light warm golden-browns and light gray when their hair is gray. Autumns look best in warm brown to red-browns (tortoise shell), and grayed brown or light gray with gray hair. Metal frames or trims should use the metal of your season—silver for Winters and Summers, and gold for Springs and Autumns.

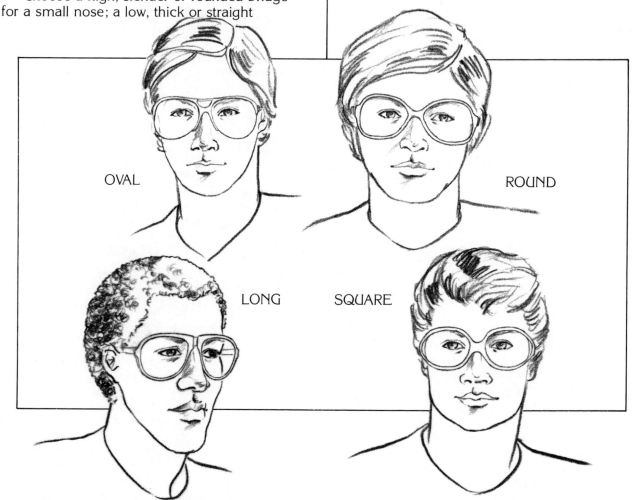

OVAL

ROUND

LONG

SQUARE

CONTACT LENSES

If you wear contact lenses, the smoked lenses are best. They do not distort your eye color, yet they can be seen when dropped. Avoid colored contact lenses unless they closely match the color of your eyes to prevent an artificial look. This is no time to get baby-blue eyes—even if you have always wanted them. For sunglasses, only ground glass of good quality should be worn over contacts.

TINTED LENSES

For everyday glasses, if you decide to tint your lenses, the degree of shading should be very light, from one-half to one point of color at the top to nothing — that is, perfectly clear — at the bottom.

Winters who shade their glasses at the top would find gray or gray-blue the most effective color.

Summers can best use blue, gray or mauve.

Springs look good with a very delicate soft brown or soft blue-gray at the top. Be careful to get only one point or less of color.

Autumns should wear from one-half to one point of light soft brown at the top of the lenses. If they are too dark, your eyes will look tired.

You might consider adding a soft tint at the lower outside corner of the lenses—a peach flesh tone for Springs and Autumns and a rose flesh tone for Winters and Summers. This is a marvelous device to add color to pale or sallow skin. Men who have tried it have found that no one realizes that there is color in the lenses. You don't have to wait for new glasses. If you wear plastic lenses, a tint can be added now.

If people cannot see your eyes through your colored lenses, then there is too much color in them. If the lenses are made of plastic, the color can be changed, and you should do so. People must see your eyes— they provide an important, ever sensitive signpost to your thoughts, beliefs and feelings.

The glasses you wear can do more than help you see better. They should enhance your appearance and indicate the kind of person you are and the sort of life you lead.

Now that you can see exactly where you are heading, let's take a look at the hair on your head.

Hair, Moustaches and Beards 10

CARE AND STYLE FOR THE HAIRS ON YOUR HEAD

Clean, nicely styled hair can be a man's crowning glory, that perfect final element of a well-groomed look. The key to an attractive head look is the health of your hair, which can contribute to your appearance or detract from it.

Shampooing, the most important step in hair care, is the primary factor in maintaining a healthy head of hair. Sometimes, through laziness or lack of understanding, men forget or can't be bothered with washing their hair — hard to believe when shampooing only takes a minute, but it's true. If you wash your hair at least twice a week, one soaping is enough. There is no truth to the old tale that daily washing or frequent wetting of the hair precipitates hair loss. As a matter of fact, daily washing with a bland shampoo is the best thing you can do for your hair and scalp.

Oily hair attracts dirt faster and develops an odor very quickly. Thus, it requires more frequent shampooing than normal or dry hair. Rub your fingertips on your scalp and then smell them. If you detect an odor, wash your hair!

For dry hair, a mild shampoo should be used.

Whatever your hair condition, be sure you rinse your hair thoroughly. Shampoo residue left on the hair dulls it and impairs normal functioning of the scalp. Rinse, rinse and rinse again.

Conditioners are designed to enhance hair appearance temporarily, from shampoo to shampoo, by coating the hair shaft. A moisturizing conditioner is essential for dull,

dry hair and for men who use blow dryers. Brittle or damaged hair would benefit from a reconstructing ingredient in the conditioner. If your hair becomes dull or lifeless from time to time or if you have split ends or flyaway hair, ask your stylist to suggest a suitable conditioner. If you are on your own, read the labels. Shampoo and conditioner do not come in the same bottle. They have opposite functions.

A gentle massage of your scalp before you shampoo your hair can help bolster circulation and release tension. By keeping your scalp clean and in good condition, you can almost eliminate your chances for unsightly snowflakes on your shoulders.

The styling as well as the health of your hair affects your appearance. For instance, you can appear more trim with carefully styled hair, without having your hair cropped right down to the skin. Most men realize that a longer look creates a younger look and is more flattering—up to a point, of course. Hair allowed to grow too long makes the wearer look unkempt, unsuccessful and out of step with the vital element of society. Hair grows at different rates at different places on the head. Whatever the length, it must be regularly cut for you to maintain a well-groomed appearance.

Many men have been going to the same stylist for years. It might be difficult to suggest new methods to him or her, or to break away even though the person's work may be inferior. But to get the best look for yourself, you may need to shop around.

CARE AND STYLE FOR THE HAIRS ON YOUR HEAD

Look for a stylist who will provide a natural neckline and natural sideburns and will use a comb and scissors or a razor, not electric clippers. If your stylist doesn't wash hair, it would be advisable for you to wash your own hair before you go to the shop so your hair will be relaxed and fall naturally. The hair should be damp when cut. This keeps the comb from sticking in your hair and enables the person cutting it to find the hair's natural placement.

HOW TO CHOOSE A BARBER OR STYLIST

1. Talk to other men whose hair you admire. Where can their stylists be found?

2. Converse before your haircut with the stylist you select. Tell him or her what you have in mind and listen to any suggestions.

3. Communication is most important. Make sure you understand what he or she hopes to accomplish, and then allow him or her to exercise judgment and expertise.

4. Watch as your hair is being cut and don't be afraid to ask questions as the work proceeds. Remind the stylist of problems you have had with your hair, such as cowlicks, direction of growth, etc.

5. Don't expect a lot of socializing while you are in the chair. The stylist is there to cut your hair, not to entertain you.

6. If the style is new to you, ask how you can maintain it at home — what brushes or conditioners you might need, and what techniques with regard to drying and styling you should master.

THE FOUNDATION OF A STYLE IS A GOOD CUT. IT TAKES ABOUT THREE HAIRCUTS BEFORE THE HAIR CONFORMS TO A NEW DESIGN.

The choice of the best hairstyle for you hinges on your face shape, location of your cowlick, the structure of your hair, how thick it is and how it grows. Your lifestyle, age, personality and career also affect the style you should choose.

The length, shape and amount of hair you wear will depend on your height and facial features. The four basic face shapes are:

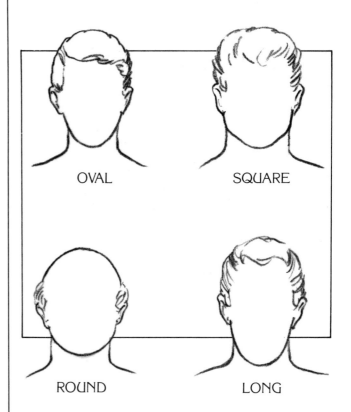

OVAL   SQUARE

ROUND   LONG

CARE AND STYLE FOR THE HAIRS ON YOUR HEAD

Oval Face

This face shape can wear almost any style — anything that your hair will permit. You can have a part or not. Your sideburns should be normal in length and should balance with your cheekbones. The standard length for sideburns extends slightly below the top of the cheekbones or bottom of the eye sockets.

Square Face

Styling for a square face is very similar to a round face as far as the design is concerned. To thin down the appearance of a square face, your hair should be full on the sides, and your sideburns should extend a little lower than normal. This helps to balance any jowly look. Your hair can also be full over the top. With a square face, you can carry as much hair as you like, and you can wear a part.

Round Face

This is a very common shape, generally associated with a heavy man. If you have a round face, it automatically looks compact. So the more hair growing on the sides as well as on the top, the thinner your face will appear. Your sideburns should be a little lower than normal, below the cheekbones, but not long enough to be conspicuous. You can part your hair with a round face but the part should not be in the center.

Long Face

If your face is long, your hair should be cut lower — but not necessarily shorter — on top than it would be for the other face shapes. A part is desirable for a long face. The sides of your hair should be full in order to make the top of your head seem lower. An oblong face presents a problem because it tends to look even longer if the sides are too short and a lot of hair is worn on top. For the man with a long face, sideburns can be lower and fuller. If you have a high forehead, try to bring your hair down over the top of your forehead.

HELPING NATURE ALONG

Perms — Permanent waves, better known as perms, are becoming more popular among men because they create the illusion of a greater volume of hair. If you want one, get one! The real tight, curly, Afro perm looks best on the Gamin man. A looser and softer curl would be better on other personalities.

Hair Color — Most men look great with a little gray in the sideburns. It adds distinction and maturity to a man, especially if his hair is dark. If you prefer youth to maturity, however, hit the bottle.

CARE AND STYLE FOR THE HAIRS ON YOUR HEAD

Coloring your hair is a personal matter. How you feel about your gray hair and how ready you are for it, may determine your decision. Outgrowth is easier to detect on a man than on a woman, especially if the hair is dark, because his hair is cut so much closer to the sides and neck. If you want to dye your hair, get it done professionally. The job costs plenty. If you want to do the coloring yourself, go to a beauty supply store and choose a temporary rinse. Pick a color near to your own on the chart, but a shade or two lighter. A temporary rinse will last several weeks, and you really can do it yourself. Just be sure to follow the directions to the letter.

Hair Color For Your Season

A graying Winter man who colors his hair blond, red or black will have a hard look. He needs to use ash browns (cool tones) to avoid turning his hair red.

If a Summer man wishes to color his hair, he should use ash browns as well, to avoid having his gray hairs grab the red pigment in the rinse.

If a graying Spring or Autumn man wishes to color his hair, he should use the golden blond rinses which can be applied after each shampoo, to make his gray hair appear to be blond. Only a few shakes from the bottle will do the trick. A dark blond or brown-haired Spring or Autumn man could have his hair highlighted with gold tones to give him an outdoor, sun-bleached look.

Baldness Or Hairpieces

Not a man alive would give up his hair willingly, but if you are one of those guys who happens to lose his locks through an unlucky set of genes, be yourself. If you're bald, you're bald!

We conducted a small survey and have never heard of a single case where baldness proved detrimental to a man. The women we polled felt that most bald men are charming and sexy.

If you're uncomfortable with baldness or thinning hair, however, you might consider getting a hairpiece. Wearing a hairpiece is a personal decision. Never wear one which is unnatural or exaggerated. If you should decide to wear a toupee, make sure it matches your own hair, and have your stylist blend both your hair and the toupee to go together.

A BIG MISTAKE YOU MUST AVOID: Lowering your part and growing your hair longer on one side, then brushing it over to cover a bald spot only serves to attract attention to the situation. You are fooling no one but yourself.

CARE AND STYLE FOR THE HAIRS ON YOUR HEAD

Ken
This young man is secure enough to not allow a receding hair line to hamper his style. A bald forehead in no way detracts from his charisma.

Jim
Jim still has some hair on top which he chooses to trim very short. This technique balances well with the shape of his head and with his closely cropped hair on the sides and back.

Norman
He is very bald on top — very shiny. He has plenty of hair on the sides and in back which he keeps moderately trimmed. The effect is appealing.

Phil
A secure man with a jovial personality, he has created his own unique personal style.

CARE AND STYLE FOR THE HAIRS ON YOUR HEAD

Beards

The type of beard or moustache you choose to wear should relate to both your hair style and your lifestyle. Taller men can carry off a greater volume of hair on both face and head than shorter men can. If you are small, cut your beard and moustache close to the face. If you feel you have particularly weak features, consider trimming your beard and moustache in a way that is sharp and crisp. If your features are already overwhelming, whether too dramatic or simply too big, opt for a gentler, less consciously designed effect.

People in the creative fields — artists, art directors, writers and so on — are the men most accepted when they have beards. Other businessmen should consider very carefully the impact of a beard on associates and customers. For those of you who spend most of your time in a business suit and must sell yourself to the public every day, a beard is not recommended.

Nothing destroys credibility and confidence faster than a scraggly, unkempt or exaggerated beard.

Mark
Beards on men with such dark coloring are overpowering unless they are neatly trimmed close to the face.

Webb
On a fair man this distinguished beard lends individuality and lifts him out of the ordinary.

Glenn
A youthful sophistication is achieved with this pencil thin moustache reminiscent of a young Errol Flynn.

Keith
A debonair devil is the impression created by this rakish goatee.

CARE AND STYLE FOR THE HAIRS ON YOUR HEAD

Moustaches

Moustaches have gone in and out of fashion throughout the history of our country. If you wish to wear a moustache, and some men do successfully, make sure it is neatly trimmed and clean. It must never curve around your mouth or extend below your upper lip. If it does, your moustache will resemble the carpetbagger or Fu Manchu styles.

Whether you wear or don't wear a moustache has a lot to do with your personality and, of course, with your ability even to grow a decent-looking one.

Beards and moustaches can correct any number of facial faults — a weak chin, unexceptional cheekbones, incipient jowls — and can serve to emphasize both eyes and mouth. Make your decision carefully. And remember one final point: If you can't keep your hands off the hair on your face, you shouldn't wear facial hair at all.

Caring for your hair should be a daily habit but not excessively time consuming. Good styling and cleanliness are the primary needs for hair, moustaches and beards. At any rate, hair care is only the beginning. Your next consideration will be to learn a few travel tips for the man on the go.

Ron S.
A contemporary handlebar moustache benefits a small upper lip and contributes to a casual, debonair look.

Ron N.
This controlled, neatly trimmed, but full moustache adds distinction to a very youthful face.

Tips For Travel

11

LOOKING GREAT ON THE GO

Nowhere in your life will the benefits of a coordinated wardrobe be more apparent than in preparing for a trip. Whether you are going for a couple of days or for several weeks, having shoes, belts, shirts and ties that coordinate with all of your suits and sport coats takes the puzzle out of packing. The purpose of your trip, the length of your stay, and your destination will determine your plan of attack.

It is not our intent to give you a fold-by-fold rundown on packing. Most good luggage stores can provide you with pamphlets replete with the latest suggestions on how to arrive unwrinkled. However, we would like to share some tips with you here from our male clients who travel a lot on business.

Soft-sided luggage provides a yielding space in which to maneuver, numerous compartments and high resistance to wear and tear. The choice of luggage is one matter in which they suggest you buy good quality, but not the best. Bags go astray often enough in air travel to make this point pertinent; it is bad enough to lose the contents of your bag without having to fret over a $350 suitcase. Your possessions usually resurface eventually, but why add anxiety to the irritation?

You need your briefcase, a three-suit garment bag with some side pockets and an overnight carry-on case for most short business trips—all pieces that you can carry with you for quicker processing at your destination. Make sure the luggage you select will meet airline carry-on sizing requirements. For longer trips or vacations, take one slightly larger suitcase as well.

BUSINESS TRIPS BY PLANE

In the garment bag, hang your power suit for business along with a dress shirt for each day you will be gone. Hang your ties or roll them in the carry-on suitcase. Depending on need, you also can hang an extra pair of casual slacks or a second suit in the garment bag. Wear your best sport coat and either a sport shirt or dress shirt and tie, depending on who will be meeting you. Dress in comfortable slacks which resist wrinkling and in comfortable shoes which are appropriate for business or casual wear. In your carry-on case, pack a change of underwear and socks for each day you will be away. Roll the socks and stuff them into your dress shoes. Underwear rolls up to pack into the bag's corners. Fold extra sport shirts with dry-cleaner bags in between to reduce wrinkles. After you've gotten this far, you still will have ample room for a spare pair of casual footwear, a sweater and your toilet articles. Many men forego a bathrobe in favor of a jogging suit for lounging comfort.

Don't check anything if you're flying. Hang your garment bag in the compartment, put your carry-on case in the luggage rack and your briefcase, if you have one, under your seat. You will be halfway to your hotel before the luggage comes off the plane.

Hang your suit in the bathroom while you shower. The steam will help any wrinkles in it to shake out.

LOOKING GREAT ON THE GO

OVERSEAS TRAVEL

Eliminate whatever you can before you go! Take whatever outerwear fits your travel style and business plans. Include three sets of nylon underwear—one to wear, one clean and ready to wear and one drying. Rinse out your necessaries each night. Laundry and drycleaning bills in foreign countries can rival the national debt.

If you travel in cold climates, consider wearing thermal underwear. It beats buying a lot of expensive outerwear that you may not need at home. Take only what you really need—remember, you will be hustling your own luggage much of the time. The small collapsible luggage carriers with wheels are a real joy if you are making a grand tour by train.

A WORD TO THE WISE

Our distinguished bearded aerospace engineer, a world traveler, has discovered that when he doesn't travel in a coat and tie, local authorities search his luggage for drugs and demand prepayment for his hotel accommodations.

REGIONAL ADJUSTMENTS IN THE UNITED STATES

Generally speaking, the farther north or east in the United States you go, the darker the colors worn and the more conservative the styles. The center of this alignment is the Boston-New York-Washington megalopolis.

Color and pattern get lighter, more exuberant and more relaxed as you travel south and west. Men in Chicago and Atlanta wear medium gray more often than their counterparts in New York and Boston, who would tend to wear a darker Oxford gray. Plaid business suits are worn less often in the Northeast. South of Atlanta and west to Los Angeles, appropriate colors for casual wear are considerably clearer and paler.

When you travel on business in Texas, you will note that the Lone Star State has a power look of its own. A well-dressed man in Dallas may give his suit a twist of regional style by wearing fine Western boots with it. He may add a big-brim Stetson hat. To visitors, this city-slicked cowboy style looks very dashing. Almost every man who goes to Texas wants to take home a pair of Western boots or a Stetson hat. While you are in Texas on business, however, wear your usual style. By the same token, the smart Westerner in the East doesn't flaunt his $500 lizardskin boots and creamy white, ten-gallon hat. That looks corny to New Yorkers.

Los Angeles can present problems in planning what to wear while you're there. Take a dark suit, a medium-color suit, a blazer, a raincoat and a bathing suit and you'll be as ready as possible.

Now that we've got you going and coming, let's take a final look at your grooming and general health—the crowning touch.

On The Q.T. 12

PERSONAL GROOMING, HEALTH AND FITNESS

This chapter presents a potpourri of things we believe every man should know but probably doesn't, things your best friend wouldn't tell you—unless your friend is a woman!

A clean, well-groomed appearance reveals to the world how you feel about yourself and gains the respect of others. Your clothes may be beautiful but if your face has neglected blemishes or a five o'clock shadow, or if you have unkempt hair, stained hands, dirty fingernails, bad breath or unpleasant body odor, then you have blown your successful image. Nearly every man has been exposed to some kind of personal hygiene information at home, at school, in the service, from his peer group or from media advertising. If a man doesn't take care of rudimentary body hygiene, he is just plain lazy and wouldn't be reading this book anyway. Our purpose is to acquaint you with the changing mores of our society in regard to men's grooming aids. We also want to introduce you here to products and practices traditionally considered for females only—which men are now using with great positive effect.

Baths And Showers

Americans make a fetish of bathing. The average American boy is a water-bug—like his father. We can both vouch for that, having washed mountains of towels, underwear and socks every day while raising seven sons and two husbands. It has long been a source of wonder to us that a boy will put his hands in the most dreadful gunk but refuse to touch a towel previously used by a sibling.

One shower a day should be enough for all but those engaged in very strenuous activity or dirty work.

If, during your daily shower, you don't shampoo your hair, you might want at least to get it wet to rinse away the surface dust. You will feel better and your hair will comb and style more easily.

Deodorants

A daily bath or shower, preferably in the morning, keeps some men safe from body odors. Deodorants should be used by those who need added protection. Perspiration clings to underarm hair, encouraging odor. If perspiration is a problem for you, consider trimming or shaving your underarm hair. Winter and Autumn men have stronger body chemistry which tends to neutralize a deodorant after a few weeks. Consider rotating two different brands from week to week.

Colognes And After-Shaves

It is important for you to smell good, as much for your own self-esteem as for the ladies in your life. The reaction of colognes and after-shaves to your individual body chemistry is a personal thing. You have to try a scent before you can know if the combination is going to work. The fragrance you use can become your signature when you find one that is right for you.

Winter and Autumn men generally like sophisticated, exotic, Oriental, woodland or spicy scents. Summer and Spring men prefer light scents and fresh citrus fragrances—nothing too exotic or heavy.

PERSONAL GROOMING, HEALTH AND FITNESS

Mouth And Teeth

Brush your teeth at least two times each day—better, three. Use mouthwash, sugar-free breath mints and dental floss, and visit your dentist regularly. There is little excuse for having unattractive teeth. If you have to make a choice, drive a less expensive car and have your teeth fixed. If caps are what you need, choose your dentist as carefully as you would a plastic surgeon. A prosthe-dontist should be an artist with color and proportion of teeth. If you are a smoker, you need to be aware of how offensive non-smokers find the odor of tobacco on breath, skin and clothing. If you persist in smoking, your teeth will become permanently stained.

Face

In addition to your daily shave, your entire face needs a good cleaning at least once a day. Work your soap into a lather in your hands before applying it to your face. Normal to oily skin may do better being washed with a facial soap twice a day. If your skin is normal to dry, you will enjoy a cleansing lotion, which is less drying than soap. Rinse thoroughly with warm water after washing or cleansing and then proceed with your shaving ritual.

Scrub

A scrub is not a soap. Rather, it contains a mild abrasive which helps remove flaky dead cells and acts as a surface stimulant. The trick lies in the gentle massage with which you apply a scrub, not the pressure. Your nose and forehead, often neglected in your daily routine, will benefit from a deep-cleansing scrub, and you will like the way your skin feels and responds to the treatment. Normal skin can use a scrub once a week, oily skin more often. Whenever you have the blahs, give yourself a facial scrub. Your face will look so clean and alive that you will feel better all over.

Toner

A toner will remove any remaining oil or any residue left from the cleansing. Moreover, it restores your skin to its normal acid condition and acts as an antibacterial agent. Your after-shave lotion is actually a toner. If it stings, though, it may contain too much alcohol. Toners free of alcohol often are preferred by men with dry skin. You may enjoy the tingle of the alcohol, however, because it feels like the toner is really doing something.

Moisturizer

A moisturizer is a lotion which helps to protect your skin from atmospheric pollutants, improves its appearance and provides comfort for your face and body. It is most effectively applied in the morning. Dry skin benefits from a moisturizer to retard evaporation of water from the skin. Oily skin needs a light, non-oily moisturizer. Note that a moisturizer needn't be thick to work.

Blackheads

Blackheads should be removed. Use a hot compress to relax pores and soften the skin before expressing blackheads. It is to be hoped that you have someone in your life who loves you enough to help you with blackheads in your ears or on the back of your neck. If you have any skin problems or blemishes which do not respond to your efforts, find a good dermatologist who understands the importance of cosmetic skin care.

Hygiene

Men who fail to wash their hands after using the toilet are terribly tacky.

Great American Pastime

While driving in your car, all alone, deep in thought, don't investigate the inside of your nose. Gross!

PERSONAL GROOMING, HEALTH AND FITNESS

Unwanted Hair

Blunt-tipped moustache scissors are often perfect for trimming unwanted nasal and ear hair. Cut or tweeze the little devils out. If you tire of removing the same ones, you might consider electrolysis for permanent removal of unwanted hair. Some men have low neck hair or hair on their backs permanently removed.

Ear Wax

Superfluous wax in the ears is removed by daily cleansing supplemented by occasional use of a cotton swab. A serious overproduction of wax may result in a build-up that should be flushed out by your physician.

Hands

Your hands are always on display and should look good. Treat yourself to a manicure at least once in your life, although it is a service you can perform for yourself. Keep your nails clean and clipped. Buff them for a natural shine. Push your cuticles back after each shower to look neater and to prevent hangnails. If you smoke, scrub your hands and fingers with a brush to remove odor and stains. Use hand lotion for that extra touch.

Handshake

Many men dilute the impact of a first meeting by a weak handshake. "Handshake" implies that the hands come in contact with each other—palm to palm—in a firm but gentle clasp. The dead-fish or the frozen-finger hand turns people off. Extend your hand in a flat position. Place your palm against the palm of the recipient. Exert a very gentle pressure as your fingers close around his or her hand. Women enjoy a good handshake—not someone shaking the tips of their fingers. A good handshake expresses warmth and self-confidence.

Suntan

Everyone wants a suntan, but nobody needs one. A suntan looks great if it is acquired properly. Use sunscreen and lotions to combat burning and drying. Be sure to wear dark glasses in the sun to protect your eyes. A man with a moderate tan looks healthy and rested. An escapee from pale-faced fatigue, he comes across as a brawny, debonair devil.

Cold Weather Tip

When you use a lip balm product, hold it in your hand the way you would a banana—not like a woman would hold her lipstick—and rub it across your lips.

Plastic Surgery

You have as much right to avail yourself of the modern miracle of plastic surgery as any woman. Consider an eyelid tuck if yours are droopy. Sometimes your health insurance will cover the work. An eye tuck will take years off your apparent age. Face lifts and neck lifts are more drastic. Whatever the procedure, remember that it depends on how YOU feel about your sagging epidermis, not how anyone else feels about it. At any rate, do your homework, get several opinions and recommendations. Choose a surgeon who specializes in the type of work you plan to have done. This is no time to economize.

Smoking

You have heard it all before, the part about the unpleasant smell, lingering odors and the effect of nicotine on the skin, nails, hair and clothing. Our concern is not so much that you might die of cancer, but that we want you to look handsome lying there.

Alcohol And Drugs

Drinking adds excessive calories to an unpleasant smell and unfortunate behavior. It has all been said.

PERSONAL GROOMING, HEALTH AND FITNESS

Suffice it to note that we are sorry for a man whose senses are so jaded, undeveloped or unrefined that he requires alcohol or stimulants to perform or enjoy.

Overweight

Fatness is a handicap. A heavy, ponderous man simply does not look as bright and sharp as a thin man. Excess weight makes you look older and prohibits you from wearing fashionable clothes. With all the weight-loss options available to you, you must find the lifestyle or diet which works to keep you at a desirable weight level without drugs or unreasonable deprivation. For most men that means exercise. You will never exercise regularly and faithfully if you don't enjoy it. There is some type of activity or exercise for everyone. Whether it is work or play, alone or with company, find it and do it for the rest of your life.

Diet

Any weight loss program which deprives you of the basic nutrients is a fad and will never result in permanent weight loss. You must re-educate yourself to eat the foods from the basic food groups in proper quantities for maintenance. We have never known a man who, having lost weight with any program which offered food substitutes in any form, was able to maintain the weight loss when he returned to normal eating—which you must inevitably do. Calories in, energy out is the only formula that works—more's the pity.

Age

"If you compare a naked man of 25—the age of peak physical perfection—with a naked man of 45, there need be very little external physical difference," writes Dr. Hugh Pentney in *Strip Jack Naked.* "If our man of 45 has taken care of his body he will almost certainly be as well equipped to cope with every normal physical activity—apart from supreme feats of athleticism—as a man of 25. And he can stay that way for years, for it is not our bodies that are faulty but we who make them so. We do this through a combination of strain and abuse which is frequently the product of our own folly, both in the environment of our work and in our private lives."

You live in a youth-oriented society, but there is a big difference between wanting to *feel* young and trying to *be* young. It would be pleasing to maintain the energy and appearance of youth, but most of you would not be willing to trade youth for the authority and autonomy you have gained with age nor for the ease of interpersonal relationships and self-confidence which only come from experience.

A mature man acting his age is far more attractive than a middle-aged man trying to recapture his young years by striving to keep pace with his youthful associates in activity and dress. Don't fight growing older, enjoy each phase. Life begins at 40, the fun starts at 50 and contentment arrives at 60.

Getting Your Act Together

The basic difference between a sophisticated person and an unsophisticated one is the ability to ask questions, to look and to listen. Clothing styles and societal mores change from place to place. We can give you some general rules to guide you in the way you dress, and we know that you will never go far wrong with classics. But to shine in your own particular social group, you need to be alert to local customs and practices.

PERSONAL GROOMING, HEALTH AND FITNESS

Your most effective reference, of course, is your own observation of what the best dressed people you know are wearing—and we mean the best dressed people in *your* opinion, not theirs. You'll see lots of folks who may think that they have it all together but who are really caricatures of fashion. Men who use clothing as palpable proof of their ability to buy—those you ignore. If there is no one you feel safe emulating, find the best salesperson in the finest mens' store in your area and talk to him or her. Listen, don't argue. You are just gathering information. You don't have to act on it. Get several opinions if you are in doubt as to the validity of one person's advice. Clothiers are in business to sell and can be influenced by fad fashions, their own tastes, and their age, but the mature ones are usually to be trusted. They watch trends come and go; they know what lasts and looks good; and if they are intuitive, they'll sense what's right for you. But always let the final decision be your own. Good clothes are an investment. Take your time and don't buy anything unless you feel good about it.

"Hi ya sol, old man, I see you're deteriorating on schedule!

A PARTING WORD

Choosing your best colors is an art. Learning to accept your unique physique and dressing to enhance it are challenges. Discovering your singular personality and deciding how to express it are fun. When you define your lifestyle and dress to suit it, you can stretch your clothing budget to include quality and class. You'll look your very best all the time. The major advantage of looking your best is that when you know you look good, you feel confident and secure—on top of your world. When you feel comfortable about yourself, you are able to turn your full attention outside of yourself toward other people.

Women might notice handsome men, but the men they remember and love are those who show interest and concern for them. A man who is sincerely interested in other people has charm—and that is our ultimate aim for you.

After you have done all you can to perfect your exterior, we hope that you will learn:

"To live content with small means; to seek elegance rather than luxury and refinement rather than fashion— to study hard, think quietly, talk gently, act frankly; to listen to the stars and birds, to babes and sages with open hearts; to bear all cheerfully, do all bravely, await occasions, hurry never; in a word, to let the spiritual, unbidden and unconscious, grow up through the common."

William Henry Channing
Chaplain of the House In Congress 1877

Marge Swenson   Gerrie Pinckney

In 1958 Gerrie Pinckney and Marge Swenson combined their educational and professional expertise to produce fashion shows for charitable organizations. Their talents dovetailed perfectly. Gerrie brought her experience in fashion modeling, retail clothing and theater arts. Marge added her background as a fashion writer, custom designer and dressmaker. Their fashion productions expanded to include fashion seminars and lectures.

Pinckney and Swenson were teaching classes on color and line as freelance consultants, courses in clothing and design for the local college and Y. W. C. A. and writing a weekly fashion column. Pioneers in the color movement and coordinating colors by season, as related to a wardrobe plan, they opened the Fashion Academy in 1972. It has grown into an international corporation with several hundred certified Fashion Academy consultants in the United States and worldwide, directed from the Corporate headquarters in Costa Mesa, California.

As women clients and students became better dressed, they shared their new-found feelings of self-confidence and success with the men in their lives. Meanwhile, men were finding that good dress and grooming were important for their careers and personal and social advancement. It seemed that the harder some men had worked to achieve academic, business or professional success, the more negligent they were with their outward appearance. Not because they didn't care, but because they did not have time to develop expertise in this area and did not know where to go for credible assistance in putting together a power-packed wardrobe. Having witnessed the success of wives and women friends, they requested that the Fashion Academy do the same for them. In 1975 the Fashion Academy began offering "Executive Grooming For Men"; and this book is the culmination of that program. The information is current and applicable to men in the mainstream of modern life. These two stunning ladies have counseled thousands of men and have yet to meet a man who is not interested in appearance or unwilling to take whatever steps they suggest to achieve the look he wants.

You have an idea of how you want your world to see you; here are the easy-to-follow rules to help you to project that image. Looking your absolute best will increase your self-confidence and sense of personal worth. Your best investment is in yourself.

INDEX

INDEX